HOW TO BE
CHERISHED

A Guide to Having
the Love You Desire

Also by the Authors

THE FEMALE POWER WITHIN
A Guide to Living a Gentler, More Meaningful Life

THERE IS NO PRINCE
And Other Truths Your Mother Never Told You
A Guide to Having the Relationship You Want

HOW TO BE
CHERISHED

A Guide to Having
the Love You Desire

Marilyn Graman and Maureen Walsh
with Hillary Welles

L·I·F·E
WORKS
BOOKS

New York

Life Works Books
55 Fifth Avenue – Penthouse
New York, NY 10003, U.S.A.
www.lifeworksbooks.com

This publication is designed to provide accurate and authoritative information in regard to the subject matter covered. It is sold with the understanding that the publisher is not engaged in rendering professional service. If professional advice or other expert assistance is required, the services of a competent professional should be sought.

Names of persons used in stories and examples have been changed to protect the person's privacy. Any similarity to any known persons living or dead is purely coincidental.

Cataloging in Publication Data.

Graman, Marilyn.
How to be cherished: a guide to having the love you
desire / Marilyn Graman and Maureen Walsh with Hillary
Welles. -- 1st ed.
p. cm.
Includes bibliographical references.
ISBN 0-9718548-6-6

I. Man-woman relationships 2. Love. 3. Women--
Psychology. I. Walsh, Maureen. II. Welles, Hillary.
III. Title.

HQ801.G6555 2004   646.7'7
                QBI03-200731

LCCN 2003096610

Design by John Buse
This book is printed on acid-free paper.
First Edition   10 9 8 7 6 5 4 3 2

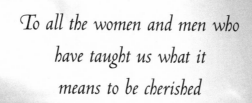

*To all the women and men who
have taught us what it
means to be cherished*

CONTENTS

PREFACE

A NEW MODEL FOR RELATIONSHIP

"PEOPLE IN RELATIONSHIP ARE LIKE TWO ROUGH STONES. When you rub them together long enough and hard enough, they become two smooth stones." So said Swami Satchidananda, an Indian teacher whose words give us a new, positive way to think about relationships and their challenges.

We each bring our own rough edges into a relationship—old hurts that have not been healed, lack of self-love, and beliefs and patterns of behavior that need attention. And when our rough edges jostle his, it can be painful—especially because we think there shouldn't be any problems. We've been led to believe that when we meet the man of our dreams, he will do everything right all the time because he loves us. It will be easy to ride off into the sunset with him, and the problems we've had in other relationships simply won't exist. It's no wonder we think there's something wrong when the rough edges start colliding!

In fact, it's impossible to have a committed relationship without bumping into each other occasionally, or maybe even daily or hourly. When we can recognize the rough spots as places that need attention rather than as insurmountable problems, we can work together to smooth our stones. We can acknowledge our rough spots and accept his. And knowing that it smoothes the edges each time we bump against each other helps keep us optimistic.

Seeing yourself and the man you chose as two rough stones

helps you see your relationship as a place for learning. You can view it as a laboratory where you can experiment with acceptance, compassion, negotiation, responsibility, patience, and love. As your stones rub together, you share the intimate process of smoothing out the bumps. Instead of tearing you apart, the collisions can bring you closer together and help you achieve your potential as individuals and as a couple.

This book can help you smooth the edges so the two of you fit together more easily. It is our heartfelt intention to help you and your man joyfully tumble together through the river of life.

INTRODUCTION

REMEMBER HOW YOU GLOWED when you were first in love with your man? People loved being around you because you radiated happiness. The love you shared with your man made life seem good, and you were sure you'd be happy forever. We are here to reassure you that you *can* have a tender, generous, warm-hearted relationship again...*and* it can be even better than ever before.

It is natural for relationships to have an ebb and flow, to grow more or less intimate as circumstances shift. Relationships need care and nurturing, and often it's hard to know what to do. This book offers gentle and insightful guidance—whether you need to perk up an already good relationship, find how to solve particular issues, resolve a crisis, decide whether to stay or go, learn from a past relationship so this one works, reconnect with your man, or recover from heartbreak and be ready for your next relationship.

You have probably been searching for reasons why your relationship isn't as warm, loving, and compassionate as you'd like. We know how difficult that can be, and we're happy to tell you that you don't have to do it all on your own anymore. We will help guide you to find the real reasons why your relationship might not be all you desire—and you may be surprised at what you find.

We will help you see that there's nothing wrong with you...that in fact, you are far more powerful in your relationship than you ever imagined. We will help you learn to use your power for yourself...so you can have the happy, fun, luscious, exciting, accepting, kindhearted relationship you desire. Not only is it possible, it's closer than you would believe. You can have it, you deserve it…and we will guide you there. This book will help you get the glow back.

About Us

Our organization, Life Works, has been offering workshops for women and men since 1984. We've seen over and over again how our work on relationships changes women's lives. *How to Be Cherished* is based on one of our workshops, which has helped women find increased joy and fulfillment in relationship. With the help of our "Guidesses," who are trained counselors, we help women both in groups and one-on-one.

Who are "we"? We are Marilyn Graman, the psychotherapist who designs and delivers most of the Life Works courses, and Maureen Walsh, who guides the development of new projects, creates and presents specialized courses, and is the business head of Life Works. Hillary Welles assists us with the writing of our books and provides the perspective of a younger generation.

We are here to help you. We will offer you a unique perspective on yourself, your man, and your relationship. We will ensure you have more tools, knowledge, and skills that will enhance not only your relationship, but many other areas of your life as well. The only thing you have to do is be willing to let in the information. This book is not for your man—it's for you. It will open your heart so you can have a deeper understanding, shift the way you experience things, and have more love in your life. You will gain skills to keep your relationship glowing and be cherished.

Rose-colored Glasses

Wouldn't it be great if the problems you are having with your man could seem as insignificant as they did when you first met?

It's natural to filter a new love through rosy lenses that make things look easy at the beginning. We all do it. It's part of what allows us to open our hearts and let someone into our lives. The love and appreciation we feel initially are strong enough to override any issues that come up. After a while, though, the issues become clearer and clearer—don't they?

Today, it may be impossible for you to put your rose-colored glasses back on. Yet you *can* put the issues back into perspective so they don't seem so huge or insurmountable. Believe it or not, it's likely that the issues you're having now were evident from the beginning—you just may not have seen them because you were wearing rose-colored glasses. Unfortunately you can't travel back in time and relive the days when you were sure your love would overcome any obstacle. Neither can you wave a magic wand and turn him into a prince. Ruling out time-travel and fairy tales, then, what are your options in the real world?

1. **You can keep your relationship the way it is.** No need to read any further.

2. **You can wait for him to change.** Good luck! You've already noticed that's not happening, at least not on your time schedule, right?

3. **You can get out of the relationship altogether.** This is an option that probably looks tempting when you are upset and angry. Beware, though—history tends to repeat itself. The issues you walk out on in this relationship may come back to haunt you in the next. It's worth doing the work in this book before making any drastic decisions.

4. **You can warm your heart toward him again.** When you allow your heart to warm,

soften, and open toward him, you allow
room for healing and rejuvenation to happen. Warming your heart is not for him,
though he will benefit. It's for you. When
your heart is warmed, you can recapture the
glow that once softened the problems and
have the passion, love, and tenderness return.

The first two options are relatively nonactive. You may have
already been choosing those options for months, years, or decades.
In order for things to change, then, you'll probably want to pick
another option. Option #3 may be the most tempting and seem
the easiest. Yet you haven't chosen it. Why? Because you love him.
In some cases, leaving may truly be the right option. If you are
being abused, it would be good to get yourself out of such a
situation. If you are not being abused, however, Option #4 is
recommended. That's why we wrote this book.

Option #4, warming your heart toward your man, is a very
powerful choice. When your heart is warm and you are open to
loving your man, you single-handedly shift the relationship's
dynamics. Your man will begin to feel more loved and appreciated.
That's nice for him, and more importantly it's great for *you*—because when he feels more loved and appreciated he will be more
inclined to want to make you happy.

When love is present, most things can be fixed. We are all human, and we are all doing the best we can. It may not seem like it
all the time, yet if we could be doing it better we *would* be doing
it better—wouldn't we? You are doing the best you can, and your
man is also doing the best he can. Keeping this in mind will help
as you begin opening your heart to him.

If You Are Angry
or Disappointed...

If things have gotten difficult with your man, you may be angry at him or disappointed in him. You have good reasons for
your feelings. It's not easy to share your life with a man day in,
day out, every day, all day. Yet it would be to your benefit to be
willing to put aside your anger or disappointment as much as possible while you read this book. Being upset takes a lot of energy.
Why not channel that energy toward having what you want? There
are a few things you can do to help yourself redirect your energy
as you read.

GIVE YOURSELF SIX MONTHS. You may be trying to decide
whether or not to stay in your relationship. Reading this
book will help you make up your mind because it will
shift things in ways you may not even be able to imagine
right now. Yet change doesn't always happen overnight.
Allow yourself six months to see where your relationship
is going before making any major decisions. If that seems
too long, give yourself three months, then extend it if
necessary. You need time to get the knack of approaching
your man differently, and he needs time to respond to you
differently. You are worth the time it takes.

KEEP BOTH FEET INSIDE THE DOOR. When things go wrong you
probably think about leaving your relationship, and you
may find it difficult to be willing to do what it takes for
things to improve. How can it get better when you're already halfway out the door? For now, step back inside and
commit to staying in the relationship for the amount of
time you've allowed yourself. Say to yourself, "I'm here.
The door is closed and I have both feet inside. My focus
is to work it out with him." You have a much better

chance of having your relationship improve when you are committed to working on it. If nothing changes after your allotted period of time, then you can decide what to do next. If things are beginning to change, let yourself be encouraged...and keep on keeping on.

BE WILLING TO HAVE IT BE DIFFERENT. This is a trial-and-error universe. Sometimes the only way we end up getting it right is by getting it wrong many times. Doing something a new way takes practice. Your willingness to experiment in your relationship is crucial.

ASSUME THAT YOUR MAN IS GOOD...Yes, you may be very angry with him right now—or you may feel disappointed or resigned. Yet staying with that anger or resignation makes it difficult to be cherished. You fell in love with him and wanted to be with him at one point, right? He must have a lot of good qualities for you to have chosen him.

...UNLESS HE'S NOT. There are a few men out there who don't like women, or who may exist to make life difficult for us. If you have one of those, you may not be able to work things out. If you are being abused and your friends are begging you to leave him, it might be that you need to do just that. Yet the "bad" men are far fewer than we tend to think. You probably thought your man was terrific at first. Being open to reconnecting to that feeling will ultimately allow you to be cherished by him again. We will show you how. We intend that in reading this book you gain the strength to care for yourself within the relationship. Whatever the case, make sure your first priority is *you*. You deserve to be happy and cherished.

BE AWARE OF HOW YOU THINK AND SPEAK ABOUT HIM. If you're in the habit of complaining about him, putting him down, and thinking negatively about him...be aware that what you think and speak matters. If you are constantly talking with your girlfriends about leaving him, for example, you are damaging your relationship with him each time, and you aren't creating a lot of space to work things out.

KNOW THAT YOU'RE DOING THIS FOR YOURSELF. No, it isn't fair that you're doing the work and he may not be. Yet if you want to be happy, you are worth doing whatever you can. You are worth the time and attention it takes to be cherished in the way you desire.

ACKNOWLEDGE THE PART OF YOU THAT WANTS IT TO WORK. There is a part of you that wants your relationship to get better—or you would have left him already. Let that part of you be open to believing things can get better and you can have the relationship you want.

LETTING IT IN

Our advance readers found that their relationships improved as they read this book, without them having to do anything but be open to the material. You will experience changes in your relationship as you read, yet there are ways to approach the material that will help you get even more out of it. We recommend you do the following in order to have the most enjoyable, heart-opening experience of this book:

1. OPEN YOURSELF TO THE MATERIAL. Allow yourself to focus on the material as it relates to you *in the moment*. That means resisting the temptation to be constantly comparing the information to your current dilemma with your man. If you're asking yourself, "So does this mean I should leave?" or "Does that mean he should change?" it will take your attention away from your process of dis-

covery. You will be making some profound shifts in the way you've been viewing yourself, him, and the relationship. It's not fair to yourself to apply pressure about a decision while you are in the midst of these changes.

2. BE WILLING TO "TRY ON" THE INFORMATION IN THIS BOOK. You don't have to agree with everything—just be willing to imagine we might be right, even if you don't see it immediately. If you have an issue with what's being said, it could be that it would support you to think more closely about the idea. Live with it for a few days, asking yourself, "Why would they be saying that?"

The mind hates to be wrong about things. Yet if we had it all figured out, we'd be living the life we wanted—wouldn't we? As you read, you may find yourself stimulated by some of the information. Your mind may want to argue with it. When you notice this happening, it is probably because your perception of things is being stirred up. That's a good thing—because it means you have the opportunity to see things differently. And when you see things differently, you will approach them differently. That's how change happens. It doesn't always take a major effort. Sometimes it just takes a shift in perspective.

Often the ideas that are most stimulating are the ones that you most need to consider. If something seems far-fetched, look at a friend's relationship to see how it might apply. It's often easier to see what's happening in other people's relationships than in your own. Once you can see it in someone else's relationship, you can see how it might be happening in yours.

In order to best use this book, try to be aware of your mind's resistance. Allow yourself to entertain the concepts that are stimulating, and know that those very concepts might be the ones that can allow you to have the relationship you want. By the end of the book, you'll most likely have the answer to your questions.

3. ALLOW YOURSELF SOME TIME. We know you're busy and you're juggling many things at once. That's why we've designed this book in easy-to-grasp chapters for your convenience. We recommend reading them in order, since the chapters build on each other. At the end of each chapter you will find a question or series of questions designed to stimulate your thoughts and personalize the information.

4. KEEP A NOTEBOOK. You'll be grateful to have your notes to refer to as you move ahead toward having a happy, satisfying relationship.

5. PAY ATTENTION TO THE SMALL CHANGES. The shifts you experience may be subtle, yet they will build. One day you'll turn around and notice your relationship is different.

6. EXPECT MISTAKES. You will make mistakes, you'll sometimes repeat old behavior...but you'll see the material in this book generally working and can trust that next time you'll make a better choice. The ability to see what *didn't* work is very important. That way, you can refer back to what you did the next time a similar situation arises. You can draw on your experience and do it differently. Often, the only way to learn something is to do it a new way and see if it works. Sometimes you'll have to try a few times before finding the right solution. When you expect that you may make mistakes, you'll be able to be gentle with yourself when you do. Instead of getting upset, you can say, "That didn't work the way I wanted it to. How can I do it differently next time?"

7. TALK ABOUT WHAT YOU'RE EXPERIENCING. The more you use

this information, the more you'll learn about yourself. Sharing what's happening with a trusted friend can help support your growth and your newfound delight at being cherished. When talking about your experience, however, be aware that it may be damaging to talk with someone who only wants to complain about men. It's best if you can find a friend who is already in a happy relationship and can act as a sounding-board or mentor.

WHAT TO LOOK FORWARD TO

After reading this book you may find yourself...

having more of what you want in your relationship

feeling more relaxed

feeling more confident

having more fun

slowing down and enjoying the small gifts in your life

having more of your heartfelt desires

getting upset less often

staying upset for shorter periods of time

being calmer

communicating more easily and lovingly with your man

knowing what you want and being open to receiving it

speaking gently and clearly about what you want

seeing a way through issues that come up

being willing to do what works in order to be happy

taking care of yourself in your relationship

loving yourself more

loving your man more

being compassionate with yourself

understanding your man better

focusing more of your energy on you and less on him

enjoying your own company more

savoring his company

remembering why you love him

allowing more love into your life

being treated the way you desire

having the love you deserve

having greater ease and grace on a daily basis

knowing how powerful you are in relationship

releasing the hurts you harbor in your heart

being willing for life and love to be different than they
were in the past

feeling more satisfied with your relationship and
your life

feeling cherished by your man

ॐ ॐ ॐ

*We suggest you use a new notebook to record your responses as you do the
work of this book. Since what you want is ready to come forward, it's important to become clear about what it is you intend. The following questions are designed to help you uncover what you want. It's best to write down your answers
as you'll be referring to them later.*

> *How do I want my relationship to be?*
>
> *What do I want for myself?*

What do I want for my man?

What shifts do I think might be needed?

*What are the trouble spots in my relationship? Describe them
as clearly as I can.*

ॐ ॐ ॐ

Congratulations…being cherished is already on its way to you.
Your willingness has created an opening for you to have the relationship you want with your man. Reading this book will bring
more love into your life and allow you to be cherished in the way
you desire.

CHAPTER ONE

You're More Powerful Than You Think

"DON, WHY CAN'T YOU EVER REMEMBER to take out the garbage without me reminding you?" Susan grouched as she tied the corners of the bulging trash bag. "You'd think after nine years you'd be able to remember just once."

"But, honey, I have so much on my mind, and I like it when you remind me," Don said, leaning in to give Susan a kiss.

Susan pushed him away. "It's not a joke, Don. I'm serious. You have no idea how much I do around here. Why do I have to do everything? Being married to you is like living with a teenage boy."

"Well, maybe I'd do more if you didn't act so much like my mother," Don retorted, bristling and stung.

"Oh, please, you obviously need someone to tell you what to do." Susan felt her blood pressure rising, and her voice along with it. "I swear, if I didn't remind you to get dressed in the morning, you'd go to work half-naked."

Don shook his head, speechless. Grabbing his briefcase, he headed down the hall. "Take out your own garbage," he yelled, slamming the front door behind him. Susan stood in the hallway looking at the bag of trash. She felt tears welling up.

"It's so unfair," she thought, grabbing the bag and dragging it outside. "Every time I try to get him to do something, World War Three breaks out. Then he just leaves, and I'm stuck with the trash or the leaky faucet or the dead car. I don't know why I even bother. He doesn't appreciate what I do anyway."

POWERFUL YOU

It's often the seemingly insignificant, everyday things like taking out the garbage that become challenging in a relationship, isn't it? That's because they point out the larger problems. Why did Susan get so upset about something so seemingly insignificant as the garbage? Because she felt powerless. Like many of us, she was busy, overworked, had too many responsibilities, and was doing more than her share. She found herself focusing on all the things *she* did and discounting Don's contribution, which kept her poised to get angry. She felt as if things were just happening to her, and the only way she could control them was to hold on tightly. The more she tried to control the situation, the unhappier she became. She ended up feeling like a victim in her own relationship and not knowing what to do about it.

Like Susan, many of us don't feel powerful in relationship. We spend time feeling angry and resentful, either toward our men or toward ourselves. We ask ourselves how we could have let it come to this, and we look for someone to blame. If we blame him, we end up fighting with him all the time. If we blame ourselves, we end up harming ourselves with criticism and feeling hopeless—maybe even depressed. Either way, we wind up unhappy, dissatisfied, and wondering what we could do.

Kind of daunting, isn't it? Here comes the good news: It's not true that we are powerless. In fact, *women are the ones with the power to have our relationships be the way we want them to be.* If our relationships are not already that way, it's partly because we may be accustomed to handing the power to men—no matter how independent we feel. Sometimes we only see ourselves as victims. We are attached to our men and don't want them to leave, so it seems like they have the power. Indeed, some of us were trained to think men are the powerful ones—even if we grew up during or after the women's movement. We might believe we are equal to men, yet there is still a pull to expect them to lead a relationship. Sometimes it seems that our only option is to respond to the tone the man is setting. We get in the habit of allowing his moods, needs, and desires to drive the relationship. And we end up resenting it.

We know from our work at Life Works that a lot of us are angry. We're angry at men and angry in our relationships. Sometimes we even enjoy feeling angry, because anger feels powerful. Yet the truth is, being angry is not being powerful. Anger is a defense mechanism, a reaction against a person or situation that makes us feel powerless. When we're angry, we lose our ability to see what's really happening, and we lose touch with our natural insight. That leaves us only able to react, rather than to have a considered response. And when we only have that option, we're powerless.

It's not that we don't have good reasons for being angry. Yet staying angry doesn't leave room for things to shift in our relationships.

Anger is a disguise for other feelings we are having—disappointment, rejection, hurt, and frustration that our needs aren't being met. Because anger covers up the feelings we really need to be addressing, it leaves us powerless to change anything. You're reading this book because you want things to be different, but you're not sure how to change them. We are here to help you find what works, and being angry at your man isn't working for you. What will make a difference is beginning to realize that *you are* the one with the power to have your relationship go in a different direction.

The Nature of Your Power

Women are the true keepers of relationship. Leaving relationships up to men can be dangerous. Men are silently praying that we know what we're doing, because they are not generally as relationship-oriented as we are. They don't know a lot about how to have a relationship work. As a woman, relationships in all forms are central to your life. Being in relationship comes more naturally to you. You are different from men. You have talents and gifts they don't possess and abilities that come easily to you. These we refer to as your female power. Because these talents come easily, you might think everyone has them—yet not everyone does. Your man can't manage a relationship as well as you can. Your power in relationship comes from your innate ability to do the following:

COMMUNICATE — You can be a good listener and also good at getting your point across effectively. When you and your man are talking, you're the one who can set the tone of the discussion and have it be a safe place for you both to air your feelings. He may not be as good at getting his point across as you are, and when you have patience and willingness to listen, you create a productive environment that can truly benefit your relationship.

COOPERATE — You have the ability to work in harmony with someone to have things go smoothly. Your relationship needs your cooperative skills. You are good at putting yourself on the same team as your man and facilitating partnership.

NURTURE — You have the innate ability to know what someone needs, when they need it, and how to give it to them. When you're nurturing your relationship, you are gently helping both of you to heal, grow, and flourish.

BE TENDER — You have a natural gentleness when you are feeling open and loving. Your relationship needs this softness like a pillow that cushions the blows of life. When you are tender, your man will respond in kind. It's wonderful to generate an exchange of tenderness. After all, if you don't get it in your relationship, where will you get it?

BE CREATIVE — You can easily come up with solutions for problems, and if one thing doesn't work, you can come up with another from your endless store of ideas. Your man appreciates your creative ability. He counts on you to come up with the exciting ideas that keep your relationship vibrant and comforting at the same time.

BE VULNERABLE — When you're feeling safe in a relationship, it's easy for you to open up to someone and reveal yourself. Being vulnerable is actually very powerful because you're not closing off or getting defensive. It's like holding out your open hands and saying, "Here I am."

BE OPEN — When you're being vulnerable, you are allowing yourself to open to someone else. When you're open, you create space for your relationship to be wonderful. Opening your heart and mind to your man allows him to be himself, feel accepted, and give you his best.

RECEIVE — As a woman, you are a natural receiver. Think about the sexual act. Whatever position you assume, you are receiving him into your body. You may tend to think receiving isn't as powerful as giving, yet receiving is actually very powerful. It's impossible to give fully without a receiver. Your ability to receive is a valuable gift because it allows your man to be a generous giver.

HEAL — Women are the natural healers of the world. You know how to kiss a child's boo-boo and make it better, and how to soothe a friend's pain. When your man is hurt, you can help him heal by being your tender, loving, open self. You can also help yourself heal your wounds from the past by being gentle with yourself. When you do this, you create more space for your relationship to be wonderful.

INTUIT — "Women's intuition" is not a myth. You have enormous powers of intuition. When you know what you know but not how you know it, that's your sixth sense at work. You can use that special psychic ability to understand your man, see what he needs, and see what your relationship needs. When you follow your intuition, it may lead you into places you hadn't dreamed you could go.

EMPOWER — You have an enormous capacity to empower yourself and others. When you empower someone, you're helping them to realize their potential. You can gently help your man be all he wants to be, help yourself be all you want to be, and have your relationship flower into its full potential.

ENVISION — Your intuition allows you to easily imagine the future—and when you can envision it, you can have it happen. You can see your relationship as rich, warm, fun, loving…or as anything you want it to be. And if you can imagine it, you can have it. When you can really see the future, it's because it's available to you. Your vision is extremely powerful. When you use your powers of envisioning, you can have the life and the relationship you want.

When you are feeling comfortable in your own skin and confident in yourself, you know how to feed your relationship what it needs to flourish and how to nurture it so it stays luscious. You can sense when it's time for something to change and you instinctively know how to go about it. It is easier to know how to manage a relationship when you are feeling good about yourself and believing in yourself. Then you can manage a relationship smoothly and gracefully.

If things aren't the way you want them to be right now, it may be partly because you have become distanced from the natural female qualities that empower you to have a good relationship. It is only natural to shut down the softer parts of yourself when you don't feel safe enough, loved enough, appreciated enough, respected enough, or cherished enough. When you are feeling disappointed, frustrated, afraid, angry, or dissatisfied, you naturally feel the need to protect yourself. Closing off your heart and getting defensive are ways of protecting yourself. When you are closed off, though, it can backfire because it becomes increasingly difficult to communicate effectively, listen fully, find ways to cooperate to arrive at a solution, treat yourself and your man with tenderness, and let yourself be vulnerable instead of defensive. In short, when you close off your heart, it gets harder and harder to access the very qualities that have a relationship work well. Problems begin to escalate, and a damaging cycle begins.

When you forget not only that you are powerful but how powerful you are, it's easy to get gripped about things, blow problems out of proportion, and feel trapped. In all likelihood you start to feel like *he* is the problem. You get focused on what *he* says and what *he* does, forgetting that you are also saying and doing things that contribute to the atmosphere of the relationship. In fact, what you say, do, and even think affects your relationship profoundly.

We tend to get it backwards. When Don snapped at Susan, she thought he was being mean—when in fact he was following her lead by responding to her critical tone. She thought he was starting a fight, when in reality he was the one who wanted to make light of the situation at first. It was Susan's continuing criticism that forced him to defend himself. Yet Susan didn't realize her own power in the situation. She didn't see that she was setting the tone and Don was responding to it.

If Susan had recognized that she was setting the tone, what would have happened? She could have stopped the criticism before it reached her mouth, allowed him to kiss her, and said something like, "Honey, it's great that you take out the garbage." Then the entire tenor of her day would have shifted. After all, if he takes out the garbage every time she asks and even gives her a kiss—why not ask him every day?

Notice women around you using their female power.
Notice when you are being powerful in a female way.
How do you feel?
Meditate on the qualities of female power.
Write about it.

How to Be Cherished

HE FOLLOWS YOUR LEAD

"Who, me? I'm really *that* powerful?" In childhood, we received overt or subtle messages about our power in relationship from watching our mothers and grandmothers. Of course the messages differed, yet many of us learned to believe either that women didn't have the power in relationship...or that the way to be powerful was to be destructive. Sometimes it may have seemed that the only way to have influence was to be manipulative. Even with all the advances women in our culture have made over the last forty years, some girls today are absorbing messages that tell them men have the upper hand. Women's status has shifted, yet our culture still supports outdated myths—that women want relationships and men don't, that women have to compete with one another for men's attention, and that we have to look and act a certain way to get men's approval. Even if there is a part of us that knows better, there is still a part that has been oblivious to our own power.

You may have been oblivious to your power, but the man in your life has been only too aware of it. In fact, there is a chance that he's intimidated by the power you have with him. He may not show it, and he may go to great lengths to prove how macho he is and how much he doesn't need you. Don't believe it. His macho behavior is a cover for the fact that he knows that he loves you, wants you, and needs you—and he can't stand how vulnerable that makes him feel. He is dying for your approval, your praise, and your acknowledgment. When he doesn't get it, he gives up because he doesn't know what else to do. He is following your lead, and if your lead is negative, you can guess where the relationship is going.

Did you notice how Don reacted when Susan voiced her initial complaint about the garbage? He leaned in to give her a kiss and let her know that her reminding him was important. He didn't want her to be upset with him. But because Susan was only thinking about his effect on her and not her effect on him, she responded with biting criticism. She saw his behavior as his way of getting out of the chore instead of seeing him as playful. Men are often more playful than we are, and they want to share their sense of play with us. Susan wasn't able to step back and see that her power lay in his need for her attention, to care about him and play with him—not in her ability to insult him.

Let's replay the scene as if Susan were aware of her power.

Susan: "Don, why can't you ever remember to take out the garbage without me reminding you? You'd think after nine years you'd be able to remember just once."

Don: "But, honey, I have so much on my mind, and I like it when you remind me." He leans toward her to give her a kiss.

Susan lets him kiss her, takes a deep breath, and acknowledges to herself that she'd been setting a negative tone. She reminds herself that Don really wants to please her. Instead of snapping at him, she says thoughtfully, "I really do appreciate that you've taken the garbage out every week without complaining, even if it's snowing outside. It's great that I don't have to tramp out there myself when it's freezing."

Don jokingly flexes his biceps. "Anything for you, milady. What's the postal workers' motto? 'Neither sleet, nor rain, nor dark of night…'"

Susan rolls her eyes. "Okay, okay. But seriously, it would help me out even more if I didn't have to get out of bed to remind you every Thursday morning. I wonder if there's a way we could set it up so that you remember on your own."

"Probably not," Don says, winking. "You know me, honey. If you didn't remind me to put a shirt on, I'd go to work naked. But if it bothers you, I'll try to remember. Why not put a note on the calendar or on the fridge?"

Susan is about to protest that this arrangement still means she has to be the one to remember. Then she thinks, "Well, I guess I'm going to have to remind him in any case. So the only way to have this really work is for me to remind him in some way that doesn't annoy him or me."

"All right," Susan agrees aloud. "I just got these smiley-face stickers for donating money to a veterans' group. What if I stick one of them on the calendar on the days you need to take out the trash? Then I won't have to actually get out of bed and remind you in the morning, which makes me really cranky."

"I noticed," says Don.

"Sorry, hon," says Susan, remembering all the mornings she's made a fuss over the garbage. She sees now that being willing to do what works means reminding Don in some way that is okay with her, and that accepting it will make everything easier. When she is willing to remind him lovingly, he will happily take out the trash and even give her a kiss. If that's all it takes—why not do it?

In this revised scenario, Susan created a win-win situation. She recognized that nagging and criticizing are not powerful. She took care of herself by speaking up, yet she did it in a way that empowered the relationship rather than worked in a destructive way. By pulling back and reminding herself of her effect, Susan changed the tone of the conversation and shifted the dynamic for the entire day. Instead of spending the day fuming about Don's lack of responsibility, she could focus on what she needed to do, be happy to see him in the evening, and enjoy being cherished by her man.

Like Don, your man is vulnerable to your opinion of him. When he feels attacked, he will retreat—as he should. It's a sign that he is taking care of himself. When he's busy defending himself, he won't feel inclined to give you what you want. More on that later. What's important now is to realize that when you know your own power, you can find positive ways to have what you want. Not only that, you can relax and enjoy your relationship more. When you are enjoying yourself, your man will be enjoying himself, too. And he will want to give you whatever you ask for. This doesn't mean you are playing a game. It simply means you're tapping into the natural power you possess to have your relationship and your life be as smooth and delightful as you want it to be.

❦ ❦ ❦

How have you given your power to your man?
Make a list.
How will your relationship change when you know
you are the one with the power?

❦ ❦ ❦

HOW YOU ARE MATTERS

Like Susan, *you* are the one who sets the tone of your daily interactions—and your man is constantly responding to you. He looks to you for cues because he is not as attuned to relationship as you are. He knows he is not naturally equipped to manage a relationship and that you are the one who can create the caring, nurturing environment necessary for a relationship to flower.

Since you're the one who sets the tone of your relationship, how you are matters.

Your good mood matters.

Your bad mood matters.

Your tone of voice matters.

Your approval of what he's doing matters.

Your approval of what he's saying matters.

Your faith in him matters.

Your criticism of him matters.

Your blaming him matters.

Your praising him matters.

Your acknowledgment of his contribution
matters.

Your thanking him matters.

Your being angry at him matters.

Your trusting him matters.

Your not trusting him matters.

Your feeling able to rely on him matters.

Your not feeling able to rely on him matters.

Your understanding him matters.

Your knowing what motivates him matters.

Your being aware of his vulnerability matters.

Your assuming he's doing the best he
can matters.

Knowing him matters.

Remembering who he is matters.

Your acceptance of him matters.

Your man is constantly responding to you. He takes the cues for how to be in the relationship from you. If you hit him with criticism the minute he walks in the door, he will respond in kind. If you give him a kiss and ask him about his day, he will be relieved and will be far more likely to give you a loving response.

You matter to your man. We tend to forget how much we matter to them. We are so super-aware of our connection to them that we often forget *they* are also connected to *us*. Your man chose you because he felt a certain way around you. When you were first together, he felt like a hero when he was with you. He loved making you happy, and he often felt he could do no wrong. He wants to feel that way now, too. He is longing to feel like a success in the relationship, and your interactions with him give him the reading he needs on how it's going.

Think about it: When you are in a good mood—when you acknowledge him, thank him, and praise him—your relationship is going well. When you are in a bad mood—when you are criticizing him, blaming him, and not believing in him—your relationship is not going well. How you are matters because you are the one with the power in the relationship.

ॐ ॐ ॐ

How is your man responding to you?

What are you giving your man to respond to that works?

What are you giving your man to respond to that doesn't work?

ॐ ॐ ॐ

YOUR POWERFUL EFFECT

Your power is expressed in the effect you have on your man. If you smile at him when he wakes up in the morning, it can make his day. If you start complaining right away, it can put him in a bad mood and he'll grouch back at you. Yet you might not recognize the cause and effect in either situation. If he's happy, you may take it for granted—and if he's grumpy, you might take it personally. In either case, it's easy to forget that how you are directly affects his mood.

If Susan knew how powerfully her tone of voice affected Don, she would have been confident that she could have what she wanted without getting angry at him. If her negative attention caused Don to drop the garbage and leave, her positive attention could have had the opposite effect. Susan wouldn't be giving Don positive feedback only for his benefit, but because it's good for her, too. When Don got more positive attention, he would feel more inclined to do what Susan wanted. It makes sense, doesn't it? She would end up with a happy guy and cooperation. Instead of seeing how she was affecting Don, however, Susan originally used her energy obsessing about how his behavior affected *her*. Thinking only about his effect on her kept her tense and upset, probably to the detriment of her whole day.

Susan is not alone. When you are consumed only by his effect on you, you lose your power in the relationship. We have all spent entire days fuming about something he did or neglected to do. And who is suffering for it? Not him. You are the one giving away your power by putting your energy toward being hurt by something he said, being angry that he broke a promise, being disappointed that he forgot, or wondering why he disappeared. Meanwhile, you are neglecting to notice that you might have something to do with his behavior. When you're busy thinking about how *he* is affecting *you*, you lose sight of how powerfully *you* are affecting *him*.

Remembering your effect gives you your power back. When men are upset, they won't necessarily address it directly. Instead, they tend to leave emotionally or physically, break a promise, or start an argument about something unrelated that takes you by surprise. If you don't realize that his upset has something to do with you, it's easy to start feeling like a victim. You are feeling so hurt that you forget to stop and notice why he's acting that way. When you can pull back from being affected and notice your own effect, you will be able to see that you've likely done something that he's responding to. It might even be that you haven't actually *done* anything, but that he's picking up on your negative thoughts. Men pick up on your thoughts and emotions as well as your words. Believe it or not, they are extraordinarily sensitive to your moods. That's why how you are does matter.

When you don't recognize how powerful you are, it's detrimental to your ability to relax and enjoy life. You may be living in fear a lot of the time. It's hard to relax when you're gripped by fear—the fear that you're not good enough, that he'll leave you, that you won't have enough money, that your relationship will or will not be like your parents', or that you don't know how to manage a relationship. When you're afraid, you are prone to holding on too tightly to what you have. The littlest thing he does or doesn't do takes on an out-of-proportion significance. The bag of garbage under the kitchen sink becomes a looming symbol of everything that's wrong in the relationship. And when you confront him about it with a charge in your tone, like Susan, you might create mischief that may be very difficult to undo.

Knowing how powerfully you affect him allows you to relax. It makes room for more ease, comfort, and humor in your relationship. Think about a woman you've observed recently who seems totally comfortable with herself. Don't you want to be around her? A woman who knows her power, and is relaxed with it, is irresistible. She doesn't have to nag to get what she wants because her natural magnetism has people around her wanting to help her be happy—including the man in her life.

Observe your relationship.

Notice him responding to you.

Notice the positive effect you have.

Notice the negative effect you have.

How does it feel to know your power?

How can you use your power to have a win-win result?

❦ ❦ ❦

ARE WE HAVING FUN YET?

To sum up, knowing how powerful you are in your relationship allows you to:

get your point across without being strident

have what you want without nagging

listen to him more

understand him better

stop expecting him to change

have fewer knee-jerk reactions

be nicer

be calmer

enjoy him more

see that he wants to make you happy

allow him to make you happy

focus on yourself more

> focus on him less
>
> nurture your relationship with yourself

And last but not least…have more fun! Why? Because you will feel better and you will have what you want. Because relationships are so central to women's lives, we tend to take them—and him—really seriously. Every sentence he speaks takes on extra significance. Every time he's silent, we may wonder what he's thinking about. Every twist and turn in the relationship road becomes a potential danger. When you're more open and relaxed, you'll be giving your man something different to respond to. He'll have more fun when he's around you, and you'll have more fun in the relationship. It's a win-win situation, and it guarantees you more happiness.

When you are connected to your power and when you are nurturing yourself by doing the things that are important to you, you can relax. Your happiness is not connected to his words or actions by some invisible umbilical cord. It's something you can manifest for yourself, whether or not he's out with his buddies. And when you're relaxed, you can have a lot more fun. Men are often better at having fun than we are, and many are also more spontaneous than we are. They aren't always wondering where the next turn in the road will lead. They're able to enjoy the moment and take it more lightly. Your man probably loves it when you can lighten up and have a little fun with him. Because he wants you to be happy, he feels great when you're enjoying yourself. When you're having fun, he will want to join right in. So remember—you're the one with the power to put the *zing* back in your relationship.

ॐ ॐ ॐ

If you acknowledged how powerful you are in your relationship…

What would be different?

What would stop?

What would change?

How would you take care of yourself differently?

How can you have more fun in your relationship?

❦ ❦ ❦

Chapter Two

Remembering You
Chose Him

On her first date with Jack, Martha found herself fascinated by his rough and callused hands. None of the professors at the university where Martha taught had hands like Jack's—working man's hands that looked like they could build or fix anything. She was attracted to him not only because he was so different from other men she'd dated, but also because he had a warm smile, a quick wit, and seemed genuinely comfortable with himself.

After several months of dating, Martha and Jack moved in together. At first Martha was blissfully happy, but after a while she found she was growing increasingly dissatisfied with Jack. She began to think that perhaps she'd made a mistake in committing her life to someone so different from herself. He didn't fit in with her friends and colleagues, and he didn't enjoy her faculty parties or lectures. How could she be with someone with such different interests?

Martha discussed the issue with Kathy, her Guidess at Life Works.

"You seem to be annoyed about the very things that attracted you to Jack in the first place," said Kathy. "Write a list of things you loved about Jack in the beginning. It will help you reconnect to why you're with him and open your heart to him again."

Martha took Kathy's advice and made the following list:

WHAT I LOVED ABOUT HIM AT FIRST

    His smile

    His sense of humor

    His irreverence about institutions

    His independence

    The fact that he wasn't like the other men I knew

    The fact that he didn't care what others thought

    The way he drew different ideas and ways of seeing
        things out of me

    He was true to himself

    He knew how to enjoy life

In reading over her list, Martha recalled that when she chose Jack, she knew he was different from the men she was accustomed to meeting and dating. He didn't fit into the intellectual crowd she typically socialized with, and that was partly what attracted her to him. Yet she had also known that his working man's orientation to life could cause problems. Whether she acknowledged it to herself or not, she saw that his difference could become a cause of strife in the relationship.

"I wish Jack could support me by making an appearance as my partner at faculty functions," Martha mused as she went over their relationship in her mind. "It makes me angry that he refuses to be there. But if I'm totally honest with myself, I have to admit that he made it clear from the start that he wouldn't be interested in attending faculty cocktail parties or lectures."

Martha realized that although she'd known about their differences from the beginning, she had also been expecting that he'd change once he came into contact with her world. When he maintained his different outlook, she felt as if he'd let her down—when in fact, he'd just continued being himself.

"I went into the relationship with my eyes open, knowing Jack wouldn't be like the men I was used to dating," Martha admitted to herself. "I liked the fact that he wanted to go off and spend time alone or with his buddies, because it gave me time to work. It also bothered me a bit that his hobbies were so different from mine, but I decided it was healthy to have different interests and that it wouldn't get in the way of our love. Yet now our differences have become something I complain about. They seem like a burden—and he seems like a burden at times. I forget that I chose him, and when I did I chose the problems, too." She sighed, feeling relieved.

Martha's relief came when she could recall how she felt when she chose Jack and could remember the feelings she had about him then. Do you remember the rose-colored glasses you wore when you were first with your man—the ones we mentioned in the introduction? Those magical glasses filtered everything through a rosy haze. In that haze, any problems that arose didn't seem important enough to get in the way of making a commitment. Yet the haze didn't obscure the problems completely, did it? When you chose your man, you already knew—consciously or unconsciously—that certain things about him would be challenging for you. When you were wearing the rose-colored glasses, the problems may have seemed inconsequential. Whether you realized it or not, on some level you acknowledged they were there.

At the time, in fact, you made a decision about how to deal with the problems. Your decision was likely one of the following. Find your response on this list.

> Deny that there was a problem
>
> Ignore the problem and hope it might
>> go away
>
> Feel hopeless
>
> Get angry
>
> Figure that he'd change and the problem
>> would disappear
>
> Decide that he does that with other people
>> but he'd never do it with you
>
> Decide if he loved you enough, he wouldn't
>> do that
>
> Take on the issue for him, hoping you could
>> be the one to change him
>
> Accept him and his problems, making a
>> conscious decision to live with them and
>> find a way to deal with them

However you dealt with it, chances are the things that are now driving you crazy about him were evident from the beginning—just as Jack's differences were evident to Martha from their first date. In the initial rosy glow of love, you may have chosen one of the above nine options for addressing or ignoring what would be your issues with him. Now that the glow has faded, you are faced with the problems head-on, living with them day in and day out. You may also have discovered issues that were hidden at first and that you had no idea would rear their heads later. In that case, all you can do is decide how you want to deal with them today.

Whether they come as a surprise or whether you saw them from the beginning, the problems you are bumping against are things about your man that you *really* wish were different. If he would only change a few things, your relationship could be better, right? You've probably even tried to get him to change...and you have also noticed that it didn't work. You can't change someone else. It's hard enough to change yourself. Have you ever tried changing even the smallest part of your daily routine? It is really challenging. That's why we want our men to change—so we don't have to.

Before talking with Kathy, Martha spent a lot of time and energy trying to change Jack's attitude toward her faculty parties. She was sure that if he could only get over the idea of the parties being boring, he might actually end up having a good time. Her conviction that he could change caused many disagreements and stresses in their relationship before she realized her efforts had been wasted. She saw that not only couldn't she change him, she didn't really want to. If he turned into one of the intellectuals at the parties, he would no longer be the man she fell in love with.

Ram Dass, an American spiritual teacher and author, says, "The only work there is to do is on yourself." Your man has his own changes to make—and you might wish he would do it now, but you can't force him to do it. He will do it if and when he is ready. The good news is that once you've begun your own healing shifts, it often stimulates your man to shift as well. As your rough edges smooth out, so will his alter to accommodate you. Ultimately, working through your own issues will free your relationship to spiral upward to new heights.

Shifting Perspective

If you can't change your man, the only thing to do is change your response to him. That's your place of power. You can shift the way you deal with the things that drive you crazy about him. And when you shift your response, you can transform the whole course of your relationship.

Following are some examples of how your response to an issue has everything to do with whether or not it becomes a stumbling block in your relationship.

He puts his mother first.

If you've forgotten you took on this issue or you didn't realize it was there...

Your response: Sighing every time he talks to his mother on the phone, resenting the time he spends with his mother, arguing with him when he cancels a night out with you in order to fix his mother's kitchen drain.

Result: He feels torn between his mother and you, and he resents you for putting him in that position.

If you take ownership of the fact that you chose your man with this issue, seeing that you have somehow drawn it to you, you can find a way to live with it, like the following:

Your response: Feeling glad that he's a devoted son because it says a lot about his character. He's interested in supporting the women he loves. Working on having a good relationship with his mother so you don't need to compete for his attention.

Result: He feels supported by you and appreciates your efforts with his mother. You've created a workable situation in which he is likely to listen to you when you have a real concern and to put you first often.

He's messy.

If you've forgotten you took on this issue or you didn't realize it was there…

Your response: Nagging him to clean up, refusing to clean his mess, getting in arguments about it.

Result: He's angry at you for nagging him, he's even less likely to pick up his mess because he's mad at you, and you get in a vicious circle.

If you take ownership of the fact that you chose your man with this issue, seeing that you have somehow drawn it to you, you can find a way to live with it like the following:

Your response: a) You decide to hire a housekeeper to come in once a week and clean. b) Trade cleaning with a chore you'd like him to do, such as taking care of your car. c) Since you're the one bothered by it, you can take responsibility for your own discomfort at having his stuff around by collecting it and putting it out of sight.

Result: He is happy that you found a solution that works, and he's more willing to pick up his mess more often.

He spends more time with his friends than with me.

If you've forgotten you took on this issue or you didn't know it was there…

Your response: Being a "victim," giving him the silent treatment, saying nasty things about his friends, getting jealous. Perhaps you sabotage his time with his friends by "needing" him for a crisis at home or with the kids, or you call him frequently when he's out instead of letting him have uninterrupted time with his friends.

Result: You're not all that pleasant to be around, so he spends even more time with his friends.

*If you take ownership of the fact that you chose your man with this issue, see-
ing that you have somehow drawn it to you, you can find a way to live with it
like the following:*

Your response: Coming up with a schedule you both agree upon
where he spends date nights with you. Let him know it's important to you to spend time with him because you love him. Be willing to do some of the things you know he likes to do, and have
things in mind that you want to do with him. Remember to have
fun when you're with him! Allow yourself to rise above your
resentment and be the woman he fell in love with. This will be
good for *both* of you.

Result: He is relieved because he knows he can spend the time he
wants with his friends, and he is thrilled that you want to spend
time with him. You've become more irresistible to him because
you've stopped making him wrong.

Do you see how powerfully your response to a problem can
either exacerbate it or transform it into something workable? It's
true that it will take some effort on your part to shift your
response. There is no getting around the fact that since *you* want
things to be different, you must be willing to change some things.
Why? Because you are the one who wants the change, and wherever you go, you take your ability to be flexible and allow change
with you. Is it fair that you have to be the one to change? No. Yet
you are the one who *can* do it. And you are worth the effort. You
deserve to be happy in your relationship, and you can't necessarily expect him to change. Your willingness to make a shift opens
up the opportunity for him to shift, too. He is far more likely to
do what you want when you are responding to him in a new, more
loving way.

Is he really worth the investment of so much time and effort?
Maybe, maybe not. But *you* are worth it. You are worth doing

what it takes to have the relationship you want. Because you do want a good relationship, don't you? When you met your man, you wanted to be in a relationship with him. Try to recall what it was like before you met him. You were tired of being lonely, going on blind dates, being set up by your friends, feeling uncomfortable taking vacations on your own, and sleeping alone every night. Weren't you? You opted to deal with the problems a man would bring into your life rather than the problems of being single. You invited this particular man into your life to be your lover and your companion.

When you find yourself wondering if it's worth the effort, remember: This is a problem you wanted to have. You once considered it worth having. And you can see it that way again. *You* are worth the effort.

❦ ❦ ❦

What did you know early on would be an issue that is an issue now? Make a list.

Look at the "Response" list at the beginning of the chapter.

How did you originally respond when you first noticed each issue?

What did you do with that information or awareness?

What issues came as a surprise?

For each item on the list, if you took ownership, what new response could you have?

What could be the new possible result?

❦ ❦ ❦

The Way It Was

After making the list of the reasons she loved Jack, Martha's heart felt warmed and opened to him again. It was a little frightening, because she felt vulnerable as she allowed herself to be softer and gentler toward him. What if he took advantage of her softness? What if he didn't return her feelings? Whatever her apprehensions, she knew she had to try opening up to him again rather than stay unhappy with the way things were. She wanted to experience the glow of love again. She wanted to feel tender, cherishing, desiring, generous, and loving. She wanted to feel like she had when she'd first fallen in love with Jack.

Like Martha, you once had a relationship with your man that made you feel alive, special, happy, and fulfilled. Remember? Maybe it was too long ago to remember, and maybe many painful things have happened since then. Maybe you've been angry at him for a while, and it seems impossible that you could open your heart to him again. Yet remembering the passionate, warm connection you had with your man is the first step toward regaining the happiness you once had. Remembering the feelings you had opens you up, making you available to see more choices. When you have more choices, you have a greater chance for happiness. When you can see options other than the ones you see now, a world of opportunity opens up—and you can begin choosing what will make you happy, fulfilled, and satisfied.

The following exercise is designed to have you open and warm your heart so you can remember how it felt when you fell in love with him.

ᴥ Remembering

Find a comfortable place to sit or lie down, and allow yourself to relax completely. Place your hand on your heart. Close your eyes and take a few deep breaths, breathing in relaxation with each in-breath and letting out tension with each out-breath. Then picture a movie screen. Imagine that an image of the first day you met your man—or the first day you realized you were interested in your man—is projected on this screen. Begin to remember the day in as much detail as you can: what you were wearing, what the weather was like, and what you were doing when you saw him. Play out the movie of your meeting as fully as you can, noticing everything about yourself and him—including what you were feeling at the time.

When you have played your movie all the way through that first day, slowly open your eyes. Continuing to breathe deeply, write answers to the following questions:

What did you notice about your man that you liked?

What attracted you to him?

How did you feel in his presence?

What kinds of thoughts did you have about him?

What kinds of thoughts did you have about yourself when you were with him?

What characteristics did he have that you enjoyed?

Did he feel familiar?

Who did he remind you of?

What were the values he had that you liked?

What was it in his personality that drew you
to him?

What did you like about how he looked?

What did you like about how he treated you?

What did you like about how he thought
about things?

What did you like about how he made
you feel?

What did you like that he drew from you?

What did you like about him the most?

What fun things did you do together?

What did you like about his lifestyle?

What was it like when you were with him at
the beginning of your relationship?

What was it you kept anticipating when you
looked forward to seeing him?

When you were first getting to know him,
how did you feel in your body?

When you were first getting to know him,
how did you feel in your heart?

What did you miss when you missed him?

What did you love about him exactly?

What had you fall in love with him?

Why him?

How did he show that he loved you?

How did he express his love for you?

How did you show your love for him?

How did you express your love to him?

What did you say to express your love?

How did he know you loved him?

How did he feel when he was with you?

How did he feel about himself when he was
    with you?

How did he feel about the possibilities in
    his life?

What did he want to be with when he wanted
    to be with you?

What did he miss when he missed you?

Take a few minutes to mull over your answers. How do you feel? Is your heart warmer
than it was? Did you find yourself smiling as
you remembered how it used to be, or did tears
come to your eyes as you experienced the sadness of what has been lost? Do you wish it
were still the way it was when you met? There
is no right way to be feeling. If you don't feel
much at all, you may want to repeat the exercise several times. No matter what emotions
you are experiencing, know that you are now on
your way to having the relationship you want
once again.

❦ ❦ ❦

Now is the perfect time to return to the list of intentions for your relationship that you made at the end of the introduction.

Placing your hand over your heart, restate each intention as a heartfelt desire. For example, if one of your intentions was, "I intend that we start appreciating each other more," you would put your hand on your heart and say, "I desire that we start appreciating each other more." Stating your intentions as heartfelt desires has your heart be open to the shifts that will occur in your relationship as you continue the work of this book.

Write about the thoughts, feelings, and body sensations you had when you did this exercise.
Repeat this exercise as often as you would like. It will further open your heart every time.

❦ ❦ ❦

CHAPTER THREE

WE ALL HAVE
A PAST

IN THE MOVIE *THE STORY OF US*, Katie and Ben (the characters played by Michelle Pfeiffer and Bruce Willis) explore the dynamics of a troubled marriage. In one memorable scene, they are lying in bed reminiscing about their experiences in therapy. They recall that a Freudian therapist once told them, "When two people go to bed, there are actually six people in that bed. The six people in bed are the two of you, and your parents"—he points to Ben—"and your parents"—he points to Katie. As the couple begins conversing in bed, their parents appear on either side of them. Each parent has a lot to say about what's going on in the marriage. In fact, the discussion between the parents gets so loud that husband and wife can't even hear each other anymore.

Every time you are interacting with your man, it's not just the two of you in a room together. It's not even just the two of you and your parents. In fact, you both bring with you a whole host of people and experiences from your history. Having a say in your relationship may be the seventh-grade teacher you had a crush on; your priest, minister, or rabbi; all your old boyfriends; the man that left you; Helen Gurley Brown; the educational pamphlet your mother gave you when you began menstruating; the movie star or rock singer you idolized as a teenager; your vision of Prince Charming; the man you could have married but didn't; your grandparents; your siblings; your best friend...and on and on. You don't live in a vacuum, and neither does he. You are both the sum of your rich and varied experiences. When you are lying in each other's arms or facing each other across a table, there are layers and layers of history between you. And those layers sometimes influence or obscure what's really going on in the moment.

It's no accident that you bring your history with you into the bedroom (and the kitchen, the bathroom, the living room, the garage, the restaurant, the movie theater, the career, the vacation destination...in fact, everywhere). Your past is with you in the present. It's impossible to be alive and not be reliving your history to some extent. In some ways, this is great—you've learned a lot from what happened in the past, and your experiences have helped shape you into the fabulous woman you are. Yet there are people and events in your past that taught you to expect certain behaviors and patterns that may limit how you perceive your relationship. Often these expectations get in the way of having the most loving, juicy, accepting, satisfying relationship with your man.

What you expect is what you get. In *The Story of Us*, it becomes painfully evident that both main characters are acting from historical expectations that are ultimately damaging to their relationship. In the bedroom scene, Katie's mother is judgmental and critical. She obviously feels superior to her husband and constantly puts him down.

"You're a child, Aaron," she tells him. "A seventy-two-year-old infant. You think it's all fun and games, Aaron. But the car doesn't drive by itself." Clearly, in her view, men are inferior and incapable. As she continues to badger her husband about his irresponsibility, Katie gets increasingly annoyed and agitated at *her* husband.

Meanwhile, Ben's parents are carefree to the point of irresponsibility. His mother says gaily, "The whole point of having a knock-down, drag-out fight is playing hide the salami afterwards." She and her husband sing a duet throughout the bedroom discussion, tuning out the difficult issues.

In both cases it's obvious why Katie and Ben are having such problems in their relationship. They are speaking their parents' truths, addressing issues not only from their current situation but from the expectations their parents set up for them about how a relationship would be. And even as adults they get what they were taught to expect as children. *She* gets a man who she experiences as irresponsible and carefree while she feels burdened with all the details of running a family and household. *He* gets someone who treats him like a child, incapable of contributing equally. Only after a separation and much soul-searching on both sides do they realize that they've been bringing out in each other the very qualities that drive them crazy from the past.

"Come On In"

Imagine that when you went on the first date with your man, you opened the door and asked him in not just as himself, but as someone who would fulfill what you expected based on your history. You placed layers and layers of experiences, people, and expectations between you. And you unknowingly invited him to behave in a way that would reinforce everything you already knew about relationships.

When you find yourself wringing your hands and asking questions like:

"Why does he do that?"

"Why does he make me feel this way?"

"Why can't we just get along?"

"Why is he acting like my father?"

"Why is he acting like my mother?"

"Why can't he be more responsible?"

"Why can't he be more flexible?"

"Why do all the men in my life end up doing this?"

…it's because he is giving you just what your history teaches you to expect.

Katie expected an irresponsible man so completely that she didn't leave any room for her husband to do things right. In fact, she only noticed behavior that reinforced what she expected rather than noticing the things he did right—of which there were plenty. For instance, every time she got into the car Katie noticed that the wiper fluid light was on. Ben had neglected once again to take care of the car. She was so busy focused on the low wiper fluid that she failed to notice what Ben was doing well—participating in the family, driving them around, and making the kids laugh. Yet how could he shine in Katie's presence when her mother's voice was constantly making disparaging comments about men in her ear?

How your man treats you has something to do with how you were treated before. A lot of that is probably really good. When you opened the door to him on that first date, he might have represented to you a version of your father's adoration, your mother's understanding, your grandmother's wisdom, and your brother's loyalty. Yet as the relationship progressed, you may have found yourself focusing more and more on the ways you're not satisfied. The finger of blame got really itchy and started pointing at him. Yet what you were really seeing was the flip side of the good qualities you noticed in him when you opened the door: your father's chauvinism, your mother's criticism, your grandmother's martyrdom, your brother's competitiveness, your first crush, or your first rejection.

Why would you attract someone who reinforces and repeats the challenging aspects of your history? Because it's what's comfortable, and because it's what you know. You were raised in it and it shaped your experience of life. What is in your life right now is here because it's what you expect based on what has happened in the past. It's human nature to want to know what to expect. If you know what to expect, you'll know what to do—right? If your mother criticized you and you rebelled, then you'll know what to do when your man criticizes you. If your grandfather raged and you retreated, then you'll know what to do when your man yells at you. It may not feel good, but it feels comfortable, *family-er*.

It's a lot more comfortable to know what to expect than to take a step into the unknown. We humans resist change because we don't know what it will be like on the other side—and we can't stand not knowing. Because we want life to feel familiar, we keep inviting in people and situations that will cause us to repeat our history. No matter how uncomfortable it may be to be faced with the same kind of intrusion, anger, control, passivity, coldness, or neglect you encountered in childhood, it's a known discomfort. It's a groove you know all too well how to inhabit. It is human to prefer being in known territory and dislike it than to face the unknown and feel unsafe.

The good news is that you can get out of that familiar groove. In fact, you may be surprised to find that things are *already* different than you thought. You just may not have noticed, because you've been seeing what you expect based on your history—not necessarily what's actually in the present. Now, you're making room for a new and different way of being simply by becoming aware that you are repeating your history. Awareness is the key. Being aware, you can notice how you react to your man and then ask yourself what your reaction has to do with your history.

ॐ ॐ ॐ

The following questions will help you identify what your history has to do with a present situation:

How is he like my mother?

How is he like my father?

What feelings do I have that I had in childhood?

What am I repeating from my past?

What am I rebelling against?

What am I protecting myself from?

ॐ ॐ ॐ

"THAT'S JUST THE WAY IT IS" —OR IS IT?

Think about the following statements:

"Men and women can never get along."

"Men need women just as much as women need men."

"Relationships should be easy and fun."

"Relationships are hard work."

"Passion fades after a while."

"True love never dies."

"Marriage always ends badly."

"Being married is the solution to finding happiness."

How true does each sentence seem to you? Chances are, at least some seem like simple statements of fact just as other statements appear untrue. Yet, other people think they *are* true. Actually, none of these statements are true. They are not facts but *beliefs* about life.

Beliefs seem like the truth because when we believe something strongly, we only notice experiences that bear out the belief. We attract toward us what we believe in. For instance, if you believe "men and women can never get along," you will find yourself arguing with any man you get involved with, though you have friends who don't argue with their partners. If you believe "relationships are hard work," you will sweat and labor over all your relationships. Yet you have friends who get along with their husbands and glide along more easily in their relationships than you do. Why are their experiences different from yours? Because they have different beliefs than you do.

In childhood you were always trying to figure out this confusing, fast-moving thing called life. Like balls being pitched to you one after the other, experiences happened to you fast and randomly. Often, what was happening didn't seem to make much sense. In order to make sense of it, you made a quick decision—probably unconsciously. That decision became a belief about what life would be like.

If a little girl's mother and father fought a lot, for example, she may have decided, "Men and women just can't get along." Unconsciously she thought this decision protected her in the moment because it kept her from being disappointed. She could then figure out how to cope with the situation. If she "knew" her parents would continue arguing, she could shield herself from disappointment when the next fight broke out. The problem is that though we think this kind of reasoning will work, it doesn't. The little girl would still be upset when her parents fought—and without knowing it, she created a belief that would damage her relationships with men later in life.

What you saw growing up became what you believed was true and possible. Your experiences tend to prove you right, because when you believe something strongly, it becomes your reality. In the movie *Sleepless in Seattle*, Meg Ryan's character, Annie, is engaged to a man whom she is certain is perfect for her. He fits everything she believes about what her life will be like. He's predictable, safe, and comfortable. Together, they keep themselves behaving in certain patterns from which they never deviate. Yet part of her yearns for something deeper and more passionate. She watches romantic movies and cries.

Across the country in Seattle, a young widower named Sam (played by Tom Hanks) has lost his wife. Concerned about his father's suffering, Sam's son talks on a radio show about their loss and his desire for his father to find someone new to love. Annie hears the program, and the story touches a pulse in her. She is intrigued, infatuated, and unable to keep from acting on her impulse to fly to Seattle and meet Sam. Yet, part of her thinks she must be crazy—the part that is holding on for dear life to the belief that she has to marry someone safe and predictable like her fiancé. Her belief is so strong that she can't even let herself speak to Sam when she arrives in Seattle. She sees him from a distance, then gets back on the plane. Back in Baltimore, she returns to her sensible, circumscribed life and goes ahead with plans to marry her fiancé. There is no room in her belief system for a spontaneous, predestined, unpredictable love.

At the end of the movie, Annie manages to break through the barrier of her beliefs. If you don't know how the movie ends, you will enjoy watching it. It will help you understand how powerfully our beliefs can hold us back—and how powerful it is to break through them. It would be great if great breakthroughs happened to all of us spontaneously. However, often we're so entrenched in our beliefs that we don't even know they are there. Like fish, we don't see the water we swim in. It's always there, surrounding us invisibly and defining what is possible in our lives. Ask a fish if it's possible to live above the water and she will think, "What water?" Ask someone whose parents were divorced if it's possible to be happily married for fifty years, and she will probably think it's not.

Our beliefs run our lives and dictate what we think is possible—yet to us they seem like the truth.

Gaining your freedom

How do you know what you believe? By looking at what you have. When you chose your man, there's a good chance you unknowingly based your decision on two things: *He aligns with your beliefs, and he keeps you repeating your history.* If your mother criticized your father and caused you to form the belief that men don't do things right, how could you be with a man who pays the bills on time? If your father picked on your appearance, and you formed the belief that you had to look a certain way to get male approval, how could you think your man would love you no matter how you look? If your father was domineering, how could you be with a man who would treat you as an equal?

The good things in your relationship are probably bolstered by positive beliefs—and these are the ones to hold on to. It's the beliefs that keep you unhappy or dissatisfied that need shifting. Becoming aware of the beliefs that keep you unhappy is the key to freeing yourself from them. As we like to say around Life Works, "Awareness is 90 percent of the cure." If you have a rocky relationship, it may be that you believe relationships involve a lot of strife. If your man ignores you, you might have the belief that men will always pay attention to something or someone else more than you. These would be good beliefs to discard.

The issues you're having in your relationship today have every-thing to do with the beliefs you formed at some point in your his-tory. Understanding where the issues come from is a crucial step to healing them. How do you know they need healing? Because they have damaged you in some way. Healing means restoring something that's been broken into something whole and com-plete—returning it to its original form before it was hurt or traumatized. When you heal something from your past, it allows you to let go of it and move on in a more open, loving way.

First, you need to be able to see why something is an issue for you. Then you can examine the belief behind the issue—and why holding that belief draws certain behavior from your man. If you aren't sure of the belief, take a good guess. Then look at your his-tory to find out why you might have formed it. Below is a sample breakdown of issues, beliefs, and the history behind them.

1. ISSUE: My husband never has time for me.

   Belief: I never get the attention I want.
   History: My mother was busy with her career.

2. ISSUE: My partner always acts like I owe him something.

   Belief: Receiving always has a string attached to it.
   History: Parents gave with strings attached.

3. ISSUE: My man is interested in other women.

   Belief: Men can't be faithful to just one woman.
   History: My father was a womanizer.

4. ISSUE: My husband doesn't want to help with the house and kids.

   Belief: Men don't do housework or childcare.
   History: My mother complained about my
   father not helping out at home.

5. ISSUE: My husband rages at me.

> Belief: I'm always doing something wrong.
> History: My parents abused me and/or each other.

6. ISSUE: My husband is a wimp.

> Belief: Men have no backbone, or men are dangerous.
> History: My mother walked all over my father, or my father was tyrannical.

The issues you're having with your partner reflect what you believe about men and relationships. Either you're following in your parents' footsteps or you're rebelling against them. If you vowed never to be like them, you're still living in reaction to them. We'll talk more about rebelling and repeating your parents' patterns in the next chapter. For now, it is enough to become aware that you are drawn toward experiences and behaviors that fulfill your beliefs and expectations. You will continue to fulfill your beliefs and expectations until you become aware of them. Once you are aware of your part as the selector and the one who expects this to happen, your responses to your man will be different.

A woman who believes "I can never have what I want" will act like someone who won't get what she wants. In other words, she'll already be discouraged before she begins something. She'll ask for it in a tone already filled with the frustration she's sure will ensue—and chances are, she will not elicit a positive response. On the other hand, a woman who believes "I can have what I want" will assume it's possible to have it. She will approach things optimistically and ask for what she wants with a smile. Her positive tone will render others more likely to go along with her desires.

Both women will have experiences that prove their beliefs right. The first will encounter resistance and say, "See? I'm right. I never get what I want." Her negative experience will reinforce her belief, and she may not even ask the next time. The second will say, "See?

I'm right. I usually get what I want." Her positive experience will lead her to continue asking for what she wants. Like them, your life reflects your beliefs. Fortunately, beliefs are not facts. Facts are immutable and set in stone, like that fact that the Earth is round. Since beliefs aren't facts, they can be shifted. Once you see that what you have is simply what you *believe* you can have, you can change it.

Owning your history, expectations, and beliefs gives you the power to let go of the parts of the past that aren't working well for you. It gives you the power to stop repeating the past and start creating a relationship on your own terms. Once you own your history and the part it plays in your interactions with your man, you will be able to stop acting from unconscious motivations and start acting from a place of awareness.

❦ ❦ ❦

> *What do you complain about in your man?*
>
> *What do you complain about in your relationship?*
>
> *List the issues. Then identify the belief you could be holding that has you experiencing those issues that way. Find the history that could be behind the belief.*
>
> *Example:*
>
> > *Issue: I don't feel heard by my husband.*
> >
> > *Belief: It's not okay for me to ask for what I want.*
> >
> > *History: My parents believed "children should be seen and not heard," so I never learned to state my needs effectively.*

❦ ❦ ❦

We All Have a Family

Lily always went for "bad boys" and spent a lot of energy trying to have relationships with them. Not surprisingly, she always wanted more than they were willing to give and ended up getting her heart broken. Every time she was treated badly, taken for granted, or dumped, she would go to her divorced mother for solace. Her mother agreed with her that men were basically "jerks" who had no idea how to treat a woman.

Lily continued her pattern of going after emotionally unavailable men throughout her twenties and thirties. Every time she found herself heartbroken, she received generous support and sympathy from her mother. Eventually, Lily found the man she was convinced she was destined to marry. After several years, however, he left her for another woman. Lily found herself depressed and devastated beyond anything she'd experienced before. Her mother came to the rescue, baking her casseroles to make sure she would eat and listening sympathetically with seemingly unending concern.

After suffering acutely for a while, Lily decided something had to change. She began seeing a Life Works Guidess, determined to find out why she kept ending up with men who broke her heart. She joined the Relationship Support Group for women in similar situations. She began focusing more on loving herself and less on looking for love and approval from men who were incapable of giving it to her. She promised herself, "My next relationship will be with someone who treats me like gold."

A year later, Lily met Henry, a shy computer technician with a sweet smile. She could tell right away that he was one of the "nice guys" she would have shunned in the past. To her surprise, Lily enjoyed their lunch date and agreed to another. After several dates, she realized Henry was treating her the way she had always wanted to be treated. He took her to great restaurants, bought her flowers, didn't pressure her, and told her frequently how wonderful he thought she was. After two months, Lily found herself falling in love with Henry. She was thrilled that she could feel so much affection for someone who didn't fit the glamorous "bad boy" image she'd always coveted—someone who was capable of real love and loyalty. She called her mother to share her excitement.

"Mom, he's great! I can't believe it," Lily gushed. "He opens the car door for me, he tells me I'm beautiful all the time, he calls me every day. He pays for everything, and when I asked him if he was comfortable with that he said, 'I've always wanted someone to spoil.' He even wants to meet you and the rest of the family. He treats me like gold!"

Lily waited for her mother to share her enthusiasm. Instead, her mother sighed.

"What's wrong, Mom? Aren't you happy for me?" Lily asked.

"Well, of course, dear," her mother said.

"So what was the sigh about?" Lily asked impatiently.

"Well...I just hope he's for real. I mean, it sounds like he's putting you on a pedestal."

"So?" Lily said. "Is a pedestal such a bad place to be? I've spent my life running after men who treat me like dirt, so a little time on a pedestal seems a just reward."

"I guess so," her mother said. "He sounds like a bit of a wimp, though. Just be careful. He might get too attached and you won't be able to get rid of him."

Lily shook her head in disbelief. "Mom, after seeing me go through all the pain and heartache I've experienced, I can't believe you're not happy for me that I've found someone nice and kind who appreciates me."

"Of course I'm happy for you," her mother said. But her voice lacked conviction.

After she hung up the phone, Lily felt agitated. What if her mother was right? What if this were all too good to be true, and there really was no such thing as a man who could treat her well and mean it? Maybe she should end it with Henry right now, before she got more attached.

"Wait a minute," Lily said to herself. "Hold on right here." She lay down and took a few deep breaths to calm herself. Putting her hand over her heart, she felt the warmth of her affection for Henry flooding her.

"I know in my heart that Henry and I can have a lasting, wonderful relationship," Lily thought. "I am not going to let my mother's cynicism affect my happiness. I realize it must be hard for her to accept the fact that I might have a better relationship than she had with Dad, and that I might find someone to love and cherish me as she has never been loved and cherished. Yet I need to separate myself from my mother's experience and free myself to have the relationship I want."

BUMPING YOUR HEAD

When Lily changed her unhealthy pattern and accepted a man into her life who would treat her well, she ran into an unexpected obstacle—her mother's discomfort. Lily assumed that her mother would be happy for her when she found a good relationship. She discovered, however, that her mother's comfort level did not include Lily having a better relationship with a man than *she'd* ever had. In fact, what Lily may not have realized was that she may have been having bad relationships partly to keep her mother comfortable. In that way she was being loyal. If she didn't get too happy with a man, her mother's beliefs wouldn't be challenged.

When Lily got what she wanted with a man, she bumped her head on a glass ceiling her family had created. You have probably heard the phrase "glass ceiling" in reference to the workplace. It became a catchword for the resistance women encounter when we try to climb to higher levels of management, pay, or achievement. Women could only get so far before being stopped by that invisible ceiling that wouldn't allow them to go higher. What you might not have realized is that, like Lily, you're bumping your head against another glass ceiling: your family way.

Like all families, your family has its own unique style that is made up of rules, expectations, limitations, opinions, viewpoints, history, and beliefs. That style is what we refer to as your "family way." You breathed, ate, slept, and lived your family way while you were growing up. And it is still with you. In fact, you may be so steeped in your family way that you don't even notice it until, like Lily, you bump your head against its glass ceiling. When you do, it's an opportunity to notice that you still function within your family's confines. You may also see that you have rebelled against certain aspects. In any case, you can see that you are defined by it to some extent. And it's possible you may need to break through the glass ceiling in order to be truly happy in your relationship.

Lily's family way included an expectation that the women in her family wouldn't be cherished. Her mother, her aunt, and her cousins had all ended up with men who dominated or ignored them. Unconsciously, Lily had also gravitated toward similar types of men. While she was living under the glass ceiling created by her family way she got her mother's full support. When she broke through the ceiling by finding and loving a man who cherished her, her mother was uncomfortable and withdrew her support.

To find out how you may have been limited by your family's glass ceiling, think about the follow ing questions:

How happy can I be
and still be a member of my family?

How good a relationship can I have
and still be a member of my family?

How easy a relationship can I have
and still be a member of my family?

How equal a relationship can I have
and still be a member of my family?

How loved can I be
and still be a member of my family?

How cherished can I be
and still be a member of my family?

How well treated can I be
and still be a member of my family?

How luscious a relationship can I have
and still be a member of my family?

How intimate can I be with my man
and still be a member of my family?

How forgiving can I be
and still be a member of my family?

Can I have a better relationship
than my mother or father had?

Can a man be more important
than my father?

How loyal to my man can I be
and still be a member of my family?

How long a marriage can I have
and still be a member of my family?

ॐ ॐ ॐ

When someone in the family breaks through the glass ceiling, it can be uncomfortable for everyone else because they find themselves looking differently at their own lives. Lily's mother found it difficult to be happy for her daughter because Lily's happiness challenged what her mother believed about men and relationships. If Lily could find a man to cherish her, it meant not all men were "jerks"—and her mother could no longer blame her bad experiences on them. She might have to start looking at herself to find the ways she'd been attracting "jerky" men into her life.

Having the relationship you want may involve a level of discomfort—for you and for your family. If you are used to being the "good girl," it will be uncomfortable for you to challenge your family way. You naturally don't want anyone in your family to feel discomfort because of what you are doing. If you have been the rebel or black sheep of the family, it will be easier. Yet rebelling still gives your family way power because you are living in response to it. Reacting against something still infuses that thing with power. Only when you can break through the ceiling and rise above the family dynamics do you gain the freedom to have the relationship you want.

YOUR PARENTS' MARRIAGE

It would have been great if your parents sent you to "relationship school" at age twelve to learn how to have a healthy relationship with a man, wouldn't it? Instead, they provided you with a daily environment for you to study what a relationship between a man and a woman was like. Their marriage was your laboratory. You ate, slept, listened, talked, argued, and hung out in their laboratory every day while you were growing up. Even if your parents weren't together or you didn't live with them, their marriage has a greater effect on your relationships than anything else.

How you are in relationship today has everything to do with

your parents' relationship. If your parents had an awful marriage, it would be more difficult for you to be in a wonderful relationship than for someone whose parents' marriage was stable. If your parents had a "perfect" marriage, how could you possibly have one as good? Even though you saw other adult relationships as a child, your parents' relationship was the one that taught you what was possible. It taught you how to talk to a man, how he could talk to you, how to be in his presence, what to expect from him, what he could expect from you, what your role was, what his role was, who made the money, who made the decisions, who criticized whom, who praised whom, who "wore the pants," who did the chores, who took care of the children, how to argue, when to argue, how to be loving, when to be loving…and on and on.

You are living in reaction to their marriage. Whether you realize it or not, you are either rebelling against your parents' marriage or you are repeating your parents' marriage. Your situation may resemble one of the following scenarios:

Scenario #1:
Your parents fought all the time.

If you're repeating their marriage,
> you and your man fight all the time.

If you're rebelling against their marriage,
> you are very careful to avoid confrontation with your man—possibly by choosing a man who doesn't communicate.

Scenario #2:
Your parents had the "perfect" marriage.

If you're repeating their marriage,
> you are doing your best to have a rela-

tionship that *looks* perfect.

If you're rebelling against their marriage,
> you may find that your man never lives
> up to your expectations and you are
> constantly disappointed.

Scenario #3:
Your parents got divorced.

If you're repeating their marriage,
> you are either divorced or worrying
> about it.

If you're rebelling against their marriage,
> you'll stick with your man no matter
> what.

Scenario #4:
One of your parents was
never around.

If you're repeating their marriage,
> you've picked someone who is physically or
> emotionally distant or someone who works all
> the time.

If you're rebelling against their marriage,
> you and your man may be joined at the hip.

Scenario #5:
One parent was domineering and
controlling.

If you're repeating their marriage,
> you are either dominant over your man
> or he is dominant over you.

If you're rebelling against their marriage,

> you are compelled to be equal in every
> thing—or you invite in a "wimp."

We are destined to repeat the past until we become aware of it, yet most of us have trouble seeing the patterns we are living out. It is often easier to see it in someone else. Can you see how a cousin's, sibling's, or friend's relationship is a reaction to their parents'? It's likely that they are unaware of it—yet when you look, you can see it fairly easily. The same is true for you. Your pattern may be evident to others, while you have been oblivious to it.

❦ ❦ ❦

In order to wake up to how you're living in reaction to your parents' marriage, play with some scenarios like the above. Even if you don't think they are true, come up with some hypothetical scenarios and the way you've been reacting to them. You will begin seeing what's happening in your relationship from a different perspective.

SCENARIO #1:

I've been repeating my parents' marriage by…

or

I've been rebelling against my parents' marriage by…

SCENARIO #2:

I've been repeating my parents' marriage by…

or

I've been rebelling against my parents' marriage by…

Scenario #3:

I've been repeating my parents' marriage by...

or

I've been rebelling against my parents' marriage by...

If your parents' marriage was great, consider the following: Is there room in my family for another great marriage?

❧ ❧ ❧

Chapter Four

When You're Hysterical, It's Historical

It was a lazy summer afternoon, and Amy was puttering in the backyard when Tim came up behind her with a hug.

"Hey, what do you think about taking a drive over to Milton and having dinner at that restaurant we like?"

"You mean Lillian's by the Lake? Great idea," Amy said. She loved the artichoke dip at Lillian's, and they had both agreed on many occasions that it was worth the half-hour drive for that alone.

"Let me just put on something a little more presentable," Amy added.

By the time she'd slipped on a sundress and fixed her hair, Tim was already sitting outside in the car. She swung into the front seat and squeezed his knee affectionately.

"Tim sure loves to drive," Amy thought with gentle amusement. Love swelled in her heart as she watched him toying with the stereo. She felt a deep sense of gratitude and well-being. It was so great to have someone to spend Sunday afternoons with after all those years of struggling with loneliness.

The drive to Milton took them onto a winding road with sweeping views of the green valley below. Damp summer air drifted through the half-open windows, and country music blared on the radio. Amy leaned back in her seat, perfectly content.

Up ahead, a farm truck pulled out into the road. It trundled along slowly as they approached from behind. Tim stepped on the brakes and sighed.

"Wouldn't you know it," he said. He drove up behind the truck, sneaking the front end of the car into the oncoming lane to see if he could pass.

Amy's pulse quickened. "Tim, don't!" she said. "It's a double line, you're not supposed to pass."

"A double line is a suggestion, not a law," Tim said. "If the driver deems it safe, he can pass."

"I don't think so," Amy said. "In any case, it makes me uncomfortable. Can't you just not pass him? Who cares if we get there soon or not? Are we in a hurry?"

"I guess not," Tim said. He slowed and backed off from behind the truck.

"Thank you," Amy said.

Eventually the truck turned down a dirt road, and Tim resumed his pace. Amy leaned back and tried to recapture the feeling of peace she'd had earlier, but something was bothering her. She couldn't tell what it was, but she felt edgy.

When they got to Lillian's, they sat at a table on the deck overlooking the small lake that bordered the property. Amy ordered an iced tea and tried to make pleasant conversation with Tim. Somehow, though, she couldn't shake the discomfort she was feeling.

"What's the matter?" Tim asked finally. "You seem a little distant."

"Oh, nothing," Amy replied.

"You're not still mad about me wanting to pass the truck, are you?" Tim asked.

"I don't know, maybe I am a little," Amy said.

"Why? I didn't pass him," Tim said. "I did what you asked, even though I knew I could have passed safely."

"See? You don't trust my judgment, do you?" Amy burst out. "You don't care if I feel comfortable or not. You care more about your car than you do about me. When you're driving, it's like I don't exist. I'm a good driver, too, you know. I know the rules of the road. And when I'm a passenger, you should better respect my opinion and my safety!"

"Calm down, Amy," Tim stage-whispered fiercely. "We're in public. And what's the big deal, anyway? I did what you wanted. You're being ridiculous."

"Oh, *I'm* being ridiculous?" Amy said, glaring at him. "I'm not the one with a macho complex about driving fast. I'm not the one who doesn't care about his passenger's life. I'm not the one who—"

"You are blowing this whole thing out of proportion," Tim interrupted. "Nothing even happened. You asked me not to pass, and I didn't. End of story. Now let's change the subject, or we might as well just go home."

Amy sat back in her chair and squinted out over the lake, trying not to cry. She wanted to shake Tim until his teeth clattered. Clenching her fists, she said, "Well, let's just go then. Because my afternoon is ruined."

"Fine." Tim slapped some money on the table and got up. "So is mine, thanks to you."

Tears of fury slipped down Amy's cheeks as they walked back to the car. "I'm driving," she said, snatching the keys from Tim's hand. And she got in the driver's seat, slamming the door with a clang.

WHAT'S THE BIG DEAL?

"You're overreacting. It's not such a big deal." Aren't those the most infuriating words in the universe? Yet sometimes when you're upset, the cause does seem trivial from the outside. To your man, the thing you're yelling or crying about doesn't seem worth that much energy. He can't understand why a seemingly small incident has you riled to the breaking point. And you may not understand it either. All you know is that to you, it doesn't seem trivial—it seems like a really big deal.

Why was Amy so upset that Tim had considered passing on a double yellow line? It's obvious that there had to be more behind her anger than the situation at hand. In fact, Amy realized later that the reason for her upset didn't have much to do with Tim's actions at all. When she analyzed the situation with her Life Works Guidess, she realized that it had triggered an extreme re-action because it reminded her of a situation she'd been in when driving with her father.

"My father was a really aggressive driver," Amy recalled. "He would get right up behind another vehicle and ride their tail until he could pass—legally or not. I used to get really scared. Once when I was a teenager, he was tailgating this guy in a pickup truck who kept braking on purpose. Dad was getting madder and madder. I could see that the guy had a gun in the rack, and all sorts of bloody scenarios started running through my head.

"I begged Dad to just back off, and he completely ignored me. Finally, he passed the guy going way too fast, and the guy gave us the finger. I was sure he'd come after us and try to harm us. I was so upset I started crying, and my father told me in disgust that I was just like my mother—in other words, an overemotional woman."

Amy realized that Tim's intention to pass the farm truck had triggered her past experience with her father. She was no longer an adult, sitting in the car with a man who loved her and responded to her needs. She had time-traveled back into the past and become a helpless teenager in the car with a father who ignored her distress. She was reexperiencing in the present the feeling of fear and helplessness she had felt in the original situation. That situation and others like it had formed a belief in Amy that her needs wouldn't be taken into account. Therefore, even though Tim did take her needs into account, she was still reacting from her old belief.

TIME-TRAVELING

When Tim told Amy that she was blowing the incident out of proportion, he was both right and wrong. He was right because she was overreacting to the *present* situation. He was wrong because her response was actually proportionate to the *original* incident. He couldn't know that she had time-traveled, however, so he was left feeling injured and confused. He was unaware that he had chafed an unhealed wound from her past.

When you react disproportionately to something your man says or does, or when you stay upset for longer than a few minutes, it's a sign that your man has hit on a raw nerve from your past that needs healing. When you're in the upset, you are no longer an adult sitting across from the man who loves you. Instead, you've time-traveled back ten, twenty, fifty years into your past—and you are now reacting to that original situation instead of the present one. It's as if you become a little girl again, helpless to change your circumstances as your mother yells at you or the neighborhood bully knocks you off your bike. Or you're a young adult and your first boyfriend has just announced he has a crush on your best friend. Whatever emotion has been triggered feels as overwhelming to you as it did in that original incident.

There are three basic scenarios for upsets that it's good to be aware of.

1. **You are in an upset triggered by your history.** He doesn't get upset because your upset doesn't rub up against anything in his history. He can be compassionate with you because he hasn't time-traveled into the past.

2. **He is in an upset triggered by his history.** You don't get upset because his upset doesn't hit any raw nerves from your history. You can be compassionate with him because you haven't time-traveled into the past.

3. **You are both in an upset triggered by your histories.** The collision of your histories provokes an argument that may seem impossible to resolve. Since you have both time-traveled, neither of you can help the other with compassion. We'll talk about this further in the next section.

Coming Back to the Present

What would have happened if Amy had recognized her upset as historical while it was happening? Instead of letting it out all over Tim, she could have taken herself to the bathroom for a few minutes and experienced her feelings by having a good cry. She could have reminded herself that in the present, Tim had respected her wishes and forgone passing the truck—and he was fine about fulfilling her request. She could have reassured the hurt, frightened teenager who was still inside her that this situation was different and that she now knew how to take care of herself. Then she could have enlisted Tim's help and support by saying, "I realize I'm really upset and I'm not sure exactly why, but I know I'm reacting from my history. When I figure it out, I'll let you know. In the meantime, please just give me a hug and reassure me that it's all okay."

When you recognize that you're having an upset triggered by something from your past, you can look at what's happening as an opportunity to heal the past rather than as an immediate struggle with your man. This doesn't mean ignoring the fact that you are upset. It means giving yourself the opportunity to feel what you're feeling in private, without blaming your partner or yourself for the immensity of your emotion. It means acknowledging the original upset and soothing the part of you that is still angry, hurt, humiliated, or afraid. It means remembering that you're a wise, capable adult who can take care of herself. And it means letting your man know you're stuck in your history, and your upset doesn't have a lot to do with him.

When You're in an Upset...

Allow yourself to remember:

You invited your man into your life so he would chafe certain spots from your history that need healing.

When he bumps against you, it's not the end of the world. In fact, it's a healthy aspect of being in a relationship because it gives you the opportunity to heal the past.

Your upset may have little or nothing to do with him—and if it does, he's probably only *part* of the reason your emotions feel so overwhelming.

You have likely time-traveled into the past and are now reacting to a historical person or situation rather than to the man you love.

Remember the original incident, or hypothesize what it could have been if you can't remember exactly what it was.

Reassure yourself that your response was appropriate in the past scenario, but that it doesn't necessarily apply with such intensity to the current situation.

Soothe yourself in whatever way you need to be soothed.

Ask for support.

Allow your heart to open to yourself and your man.

Becoming aware of the real reason you're upset begins the healing process. Every time you are aware that your upset is historical, you create room for healing to happen. Old hurt, anger, pain, fear, humiliation, and sadness clog up your heart so you can't love fully in the present. Every issue you heal creates more space for love in your heart. The more space you have for love, the better your relationship will be and the happier you will become.

❧ ❧ ❧

What upsets did you have with your man recently?

What history did each of these upsets evoke?

How can you help the part of you that still gets upset in that kind of incident?

Imagine telling your partner that the strength of your response was stimulated by the past experience you uncovered.

What happens when you answer the above questions?

❧ ❧ ❧

WHEN YOU'RE BOTH HYSTERICAL

"That was the funniest movie I've seen in a long time," Brian said to Jeannie as they left the theater.

"Oh, I know; wasn't it great?" Jeannie agreed.

Brian stopped suddenly and his hand went rigid in Jeannie's.

She looked up, surprised. "What's the matter?" she asked.

Jeannie followed Brian's gaze toward two teenagers locked in an embrace in the parking lot. The girl looked familiar, her blond ponytail illuminated by a streetlight. In fact, the jacket she was wearing was exactly like the one Jeannie had just bought for their sixteen-year-old daughter, Val.

"That girl looks like Val, doesn't she?" Jeannie said.

"Jeannie, that *is* Val," said Brian.

"No, it's not. It couldn't be. She's over at her friend Tina's watching videos tonight."

The teenagers parted for a moment, staring into each other's eyes, and Jeannie saw the girl's face.

"Oh my, you're right," breathed Jeannie. She tugged at Brian's hand. "Come on, honey, let's go. She'll be embarrassed if they see us."

Brian dropped Jeannie's hand impatiently. "What are you talking about? I'm going over there to put a stop to this."

"No!" Jeannie hissed. "Come on, Brian, it's not like they're naked or anything. It's an innocent kiss in a public place. That must be that boy Keith she's been telling us about. Oh, he's a cute one, isn't he? See his letter jacket? He's the captain of the soccer team."

Brian stared at Jeannie. "I cannot believe you're standing there talking about how cute this guy is when not only is he kissing our daughter, but she lied to us about where she was going tonight. She knows I won't allow her to go out with boys alone. We've been through this a hundred times."

"Yes, and for the hundredth time, she's a junior in high school, Brian. She's sixteen. All the other girls her age are allowed to go out with boys, and it's not fair to keep her under such strict rules. Let her have some fun. She's a straight-A student and a good athlete. It's not like she's going to get into trouble. She has a good head on her shoulders."

"Listen, Jeannie, I'm not going to let you intervene for her when she's blatantly broken a rule *and* lied to us. She's in big trouble."

"She's a good kid, Brian! I will not have my daughter subjected to arbitrary rules like I was at her age. I wasn't even allowed to go out with my friends, never mind boys. It was awful. I can't tell you how many nights I cried myself to sleep because I had to miss a party or a dance. You're only young once, and I want our daughter to have a happy high-school experience."

"Well, I'm sorry you had such a rotten time, but you were better off than my sister. I won't have Val getting into trouble like Holly did."

Jeannie sighed in exasperation. "Just because your sister got pregnant at sixteen doesn't have anything to do with our daughter. How many times have we been over this, Brian? Val is not going to mess up her life. She already knows what college she wants to go to, for goodness' sake. Your sister had problems. Val is nothing like her."

Brian just shook his head and started walking toward Val and the boy, who were talking with their arms around each other and seemed oblivious to anything going on around them. Jeannie darted after him.

"Stop!" she commanded, grasping for the back of Brian's jacket. He ignored her.

"Valerie," he called in a stern voice, striding toward the teens. She looked up and Jeannie saw shock register on her face as she recognized her parents coming toward her.

"Come with us right now," Brian said.

"It's okay, sir, we weren't doing anything," said Keith.

"You be quiet and leave my daughter alone," said Brian. "If I ever catch you with her again, you'll regret it for the rest of your life."

"Oh, Brian, don't overreact," said Jeannie. She turned her back on him and put her arm around Val, who had started to cry. Jeannie walked her to their car.

"I'm sorry, Mom and Dad," Val said as she got into the back seat. She hiccuped. "It's just that I really, really like Keith and he really likes me. And I knew there was no way you'd let me go out with him. I'm sorry I lied to you, really I am."

"See, Brian?" Jeannie said as he started the car. "If you'd just let her go out, she wouldn't have to go behind our backs. She doesn't *want* to have to lie to us. You forced her into this position."

"That's enough from both of you," Brian said. "I don't want to hear any more about it. Val, you broke the rules and lied to us. That's the end of the story. You're grounded for the rest of the semester." He turned on the radio and cranked up the volume. Jeannie folded her arms and sighed, scooting as far away from him as she could. They drove home without saying another word.

PIECING IT TOGETHER

Why couldn't Jeannie and Brian resolve their argument? Because they were *both* in upsets triggered by their histories at the same time. Brian was reliving the time when his teenage sister's pregnancy tore his family apart, and Jeannie was reliving her own teen years when she was kept cloistered by overly strict parents. Since both of them had time-traveled into the past, neither was present in the moment to help the other find resolution.

Imagine for a moment that life is a jigsaw puzzle and people are the puzzle pieces. Each piece is unique. Its shape is determined by the history, beliefs, expectations, talents, interests, and desires of the individual. The pieces can fit in only with other pieces whose shape corresponds to their own. The pieces connect because they can give each other the stimulation they need in order to heal the past.

Jeannie and Brian's argument was a result of the way their puzzle pieces fit together. Brian was a puzzle piece shaped, "My daughter isn't safe unless I keep her under strict supervision." Jeannie was a puzzle piece shaped, "I want my daughter to have the freedom I never had." Their puzzle pieces fit each other's perfectly because they touched each other in the spots that each of them needed to heal from the past.

You and your man also fit each other like puzzle pieces. In fact, you chose him partly because his puzzle piece fits yours. His piece is perfectly formed to fit yours because it matches what you need to heal in your life. When only one of you gets triggered by your history, the other one can be available to help with the problem. But when you are both time-traveling into the past, that's when an explosion can happen.

> If your puzzle piece is shaped, "Men always love someone more than me"…you may attract a mate whose piece is shaped, "Women never feel I love them enough" or "Women want too much from me."

> If your puzzle piece is shaped, "I can't get loved enough"…you may find a partner whose piece is shaped, "It's too uncomfortable to get close."

> If your puzzle piece is shaped, "I can't get my way"…his may be, "No one will tell me what to do."

> If your puzzle piece is shaped, "I'm afraid of someone getting close to me"…you may end up with a man whose piece is shaped, "I'm too busy to spend time with you."

Your puzzle piece and your man's puzzle piece are formed to fit together perfectly. He fulfills what you believe and expect based on your history. In fact, you draw out of him the behavior that reinforces your beliefs and expectations. However he's behaving, you see what you expect. Like a rough stone, he chafes you in many of the spots you need to be chafed in order to heal the past and create more room for love in your heart. And he's not the first one to fit your piece of the puzzle. Other men you've been involved with probably have the same issues. It may not look that way on the surface. The names, faces, and circumstances are different—yet the issues have been there all along. And the issues you have create certain scenarios with men, over and over.

"I've Never Acted This Way Before..."

When Brian, Jeannie, and Val got home from the movie theater, Jeannie grabbed her pillow and a blanket off the bed and took them to the den. Furious, she couldn't face sleeping next to Brian all night. She lay down on the sofa, staring at the ceiling.

After a few minutes, Brian came in. "Are you coming to bed?" he asked.

"No," Jeannie said.

"Why not?"

"Because I'm angry at you," Jeannie said.

"Come on, Jeannie. Let's not do this. I'm just reinforcing the rules we both set up."

"No. You set them up over my protests. You never listen to me. I might as well not say anything at all." And Jeannie turned to face the back of the sofa.

Brian sighed. "Please come to bed. Can't we just agree to disagree on this?"

"No," said Jeannie.

"Arrrggghh!" Brian let out a frustrated yell, grabbing his hair with both hands.

Jeannie just lay there, wishing he would go away.

Brian grabbed her blanket off. "Come upstairs right now!"

Jeannie sat up. "You can be such a tyrant, Brian."

"It's your fault. You make me act like this. I never *used* to be a tyrant. You drive me to the brink!" Maddened with frustration, Brian threw the blanket across the room and stomped out.

Have you ever had a man say to you, "I've never acted this way with a woman before!" Just as Jeannie pulled certain behavior out of Brian, you pull certain behaviors from your man because they are the ones that fit your puzzle piece. Jeannie expected Brian to be domineering like her parents, and she perceived his actions through the lens of her expectation. Like Jeannie, you expect your man to be a certain way. Then you do things that pull him to act that way—or at least you perceive that he does. You receive his actions in the light of what you expect. It's as if by expecting him to be a certain way, you create him in the image of your expectation.

Brian might have acted differently with someone other than Jeannie because she would have had a different history. You draw men to you that chafe what hasn't been healed—and like Jeannie, or Amy in the previous chapter, you will continue to draw the same things from men until those issues are healed. If you don't work on it now with your man, the issues won't just magically go away. They'll still be there with the next man, with your boss, your friends, or your next-door neighbor.

The Healing Begins

What would it be like if you could see your disagreements as opportunities you've invited into your life? If Jeannie could look this way, she would see that what needs healing is not her current relationship, but her anger at her parents. She could say to herself, "I'm forty-five years old and now have a say in what happens. It doesn't have to be like my childhood anymore. I can see I'm pushing against Brian as a reaction against my parents—not necessarily as a reaction to him." If Brian could look for his healing opportunity, he could say, "I need to heal my feelings of helplessness. I couldn't help my sister, but I have power with my daughter and I don't have to be so strict to keep her safe."

What if you knew that when he annoys you, frustrates you, pushes your buttons, disappoints you...he is giving you the opportunity to heal in just the way you need to? Instead of pointing an accusatory finger, you could be grateful to him for stimulating your healing process. Imagine how that shift would change the dynamics of your relationship.

When you chafe each other's wounds from the past, it feels bad. It brings up a lot of strong emotions, thoughts, body sensations, and memories. And no one likes to feel bad. It's natural to want to get rid of the feeling as soon as possible, often by blaming it on the one who brought on the upset. In order to heal, though, it's important to be willing to be uncomfortable. Feeling bad is a necessary part of healing, like the pain or itchiness of a cut healing on your finger. If you decide to go on a health program, it might feel really bad to go to the gym at first. You might hate the outfits, the fact that you have to put the StairMaster on Level I, and the pain in your legs after finishing a workout. Yet, if you're willing to go through that discomfort, you begin to get results. Eventually, it doesn't feel so bad—and you might even begin feeling better than you ever have.

Sometimes it's necessary to feel bad so a good thing can happen. Next time you find yourself really upset, ask yourself: "What wants to be healed?"

If you feel angry, you have the opportunity to go back into the past and find out who the original person is that you're mad at. If you feel sad, you can grieve for the original sadness. If you feel humiliated, you can reassure yourself that you lived through it and you no longer need to be embarrassed. If you feel hurt, you can soothe the part of you that's still wounded. Once you allow yourself to feel bad, the healing process has begun.

த் த் த்

> Allow yourself to acknowledge that you unknowingly invited your man into your life so you can repeat issues in your past that need healing.
>
> What might these issues be? Make a list.
>
> What wants to be healed?

த் த் த்

Metamorphosis

A shift in perspective is often the only catalyst needed to stimulate healing. It's like tilting your head to see the world at a slightly different angle. When you start seeing your relationship as a place for healing, it begins to shift. Like the ever-changing form of an amoeba, the shape of your puzzle piece changes as you heal. Your man's puzzle piece will shift to accommodate your new shape, and your relationship will take on a fresh, flexible form. Every time you heal a bit of your past, your heart opens more. As your heart opens more, your man will respond differently and your relationship will shift slightly. This doesn't mean that issues won't come up. It does mean that you'll be dealing with them in a way that benefits you, your man, and your relationship.

Healing Yourself

Admit that the issue has something to do with you because it happens to you in a variety of ways, over and over.

Own that the issue has something to do with you because you may be upset out of proportion to the incident, or because you stay upset for more than a few minutes.

Acknowledge that the issue is causing you to repeat your history in some way.

Realize that unknowingly you chose this man because he has you repeating your past.

Ask, "Who does he remind me of from my past?"

Recognize that the thoughts, feelings, and body sensations you're having in your current upset are the same ones you experienced as a child, teenager, or young adult—even if you don't have a clear recollection of the past.

See that you have probably had this same issue with other people in your life. The names have changed, the circumstances have changed, but the issue is still the same.

Acknowledge that the issue has shown up so you can heal it.

As we've said before, awareness is 90 percent of the cure. Simply recognizing that an upset is historical and that your man is in your life to help you heal it, is enough to change the entire tone of your relationship. Being willing to see your issues and keep your heart open to your man changes the vibration you're giving off. Instead of, "You're driving me crazy and I don't know if I want to put up with this anymore," you will be sending out, "I'm upset right now and it doesn't have a lot to do with you." Instead of "Why can't you just be different?" you'll be sending out, "My heart is open to you and I have issues I need to work out on my own right now." When you shift your energy toward healing and away from blaming, your man will experience you differently and he will be a lot more willing to give you what you want.

❧ Ways to Heal

Become aware. Often, this is all you need to do to begin a profound shift.

Observe what your man is doing to stimulate your healing. Instead of getting upset with him, you can say, "Here is my man doing his job. I hired him to bring my history forward so it could be healed, and he's doing a great job of it. He's giving me another opportunity to learn about myself."

Find the past circumstances that are being repeated. Hypothesize if you can't recall them specifically. Ask yourself,

What did I need then?

What solution would have worked? Think of two or three options.

What do I know now I didn't know then?

What can I do for myself now?

What support can I ask for now?

Notice that your response to him is more about your history than it is about the man in your life. It may look like him standing there, but the enormity of your upset can clue you in to the fact that you're actually facing your mother, your father, your fifth-grade teacher, your grandparent, your aunt, your uncle, your older sibling, or an old boyfriend.

Ask yourself, "How can I respond differently?"

Give him something different to respond to. When you change your vibration, he will be responding to your increased awareness that you are repeating old patterns—and therefore your increased openheartedness, care, and love.

Notice that it is easier to love him when you find what needs to be healed in the past and begin to heal it. Try behaving differently with him than you usually do. See how he responds when you behave in a more loving way.

❦ ❦ ❦

As we mentioned in the introduction, sometimes you need a cheerleading section as you go bravely into your healing. To support yourself in the process, it works well to find one or more of the following:

> A diary for recording your thoughts, feelings, body sensations, revelations, challenges, and joys

> A good friend who understands what you're doing and will be there when you need positive reinforcement

> A mentor—a woman who has a relationship you admire and who can be an inspiration for you

> A therapist or Guidess who will help you delve more deeply into your childhood issues and assist in your healing process

> A conscious group of women who are taking responsibility for their lives and relationships, who meet regularly to share their experiences

> Do the exercises above using recent upsets.

❦ ❦ ❦

CHAPTER FIVE

THE KEY TO BEING CHERISHED

TIRED OF DINNERS GETTING COLD and late-night worrying sessions, Heidi decided something had to change.

"I'm sick of wondering whether or not Stuart is coming home to dinner," she said to herself. "I realize we're committed to letting each other have our freedom, but I have limits. I'm tired of waking up late at night when my husband's gone out and worrying about him."

Heidi decided to ask Stuart to start calling her if he knew he'd be late getting home. She waited for a time when they were both in a good mood, then explained that it was an inconvenience not to know when he would arrive at the house—whether she was at work planning what they'd have for dinner or at home while he was out with his friends.

"Could you call me ahead of time to let me know your plans?" Heidi asked.

Stuart agreed. A few days later, he called her office at 4:30 to tell her he wouldn't be home for dinner.

"A client flew into town today, and I have to take him out," he explained.

"What!" Heidi burst out. "Why didn't you tell me earlier? I went out on my lunch break and bought fish that has to be eaten tonight."

"Oh, sorry," Stuart said. "I didn't realize you'd gone shopping. Um, you asked me to call when I knew I had dinner plans, so I did."

Heidi tapped her fingernails on her desk impatiently. "Stu, you can't just call me at the last minute. I have to plan ahead, you know. Now the fish will spoil. Well, have a good dinner." She hung up.

When Stuart got home that evening, he went straight past Heidi into the bedroom without saying hello. Heidi followed him, realizing she'd been a little hard on him earlier. She apologized for hanging up and admitted she'd been hasty.

"But I need you to let me know as soon as you can in the day what your plans are, so I don't waste time and effort on dinner. If you're not here, I'm happy to just have leftovers or cheese and crackers."

"Okay, I'll try to let you know earlier," Stuart sighed.

The following Thursday morning, Stuart told Heidi he and his buddy were going to the Nicks game the next night.

"Great, I hope you have fun," said Heidi. "I'm beat, I've had a really stressful week at work. I'll just stay home and relax."

Friday evening Heidi picked up some takeout sushi and a magazine. After eating, she ran herself a hot bath and sank gratefully into the bubbles to read about the latest fashions. By nine o'clock, she was comfortably ensconced in their bed and fell into a deep, luxurious sleep.

The phone's ring startled her awake, heart pounding. She glanced at the clock, saw that it was nearly midnight, and ran to the living room to answer the phone. She was sure something was horribly wrong.

"Hi honey, it's me." Stu was shouting over a babble of background noise. "The Nicks won, and we're out celebrating. Just wanted to let you know I won't be home till late, and not to worry."

Heidi put her hand on her racing heart. "Stu, you scared the daylights out of me. What time is it? Why are you calling in the middle of the night?"

"Because you told me you want to know when I'll be late so you don't worry. Remember?" said Stu, exasperated.

Heidi clenched her teeth. "I can't believe you woke me out of a sound sleep for this when you know I've had such an exhausting week. Now I'll probably never get back to sleep."

For a moment, all she could hear was music blaring and men's voices shouting. Finally Stu said, "Yeah. Well, gotta go," and hung up.

Heidi stared at the phone. "I can't believe he hung up on me," she said to herself. Too upset to go back to sleep, she made herself a cup of cocoa and sat in the dark living room for what seemed like ages. When the clock struck two, she finally stumbled to bed and fell into a fitful slumber.

The next morning, Heidi awoke feeling hurt and angry. She waited for Stuart to wake up and immediately began questioning him about the previous night.

"I can't believe you hung up on me. Why did you do that? What time did you get home? What were you and your buddies doing until all hours?"

"Gosh, Heidi, let me at least wake up first," said Stuart. He shook her arm off and stomped into the bathroom. When he emerged after a shower, Heidi tried questioning him again.

"I was just out with my friends. Since when do I need to answer to a cross-examination?" he muttered. "I'm going out to get a cup of coffee."

After that, things got increasingly strained between Heidi and Stuart. Every time they talked about his plans, they got in an argument, and eventually Stuart stopped calling ahead to let her know what he was doing. Heidi felt increasingly hurt and neglected, and her attempts to talk to Stuart about the situation almost always ended in an impasse. He started spending more time away from home, and they didn't seem to have any fun together anymore. Heidi began to wonder if their marriage was going to last. It sure seemed as if things were headed down a slippery slope.

FINDING HER PART

Let's freeze Stuart and Heidi's drama at this moment. Things are moving in a downward spiral, and both Heidi and Stuart are frustrated. He feels criticized and blamed by Heidi, and she feels angry that he's not willing to communicate with her.

What can Heidi do to turn the situation around?

I. SHE CAN REMEMBER THAT AS A WOMAN, SHE HAS POWER IN HER RELATIONSHIP. She is the one who sets the tone, and

Stuart responds to it—not the other way around. Remembering her power will allow her to relax because she will be able to see that she's not trapped. There *is* something she can do to change the way things are headed. She doesn't have to be his victim.

2. SHE CAN BE WILLING TO LISTEN TO—AND *HEAR*—STUART'S SIDE OF THE ISSUE. We all know how difficult it can be to really hear another's side of the story, especially when we're upset. Yet we can see that it's crucial at this point for Heidi to listen to Stuart and acknowledge that he has a valid point of view—even if she doesn't understand it.

Heidi's first reaction to Stuart's account of events might be to discount what he says. "How could he possibly think that? That's not the way it is." Yet when she is willing to hear him and put herself in his shoes for a moment, she will remember that there is no right or wrong perception of what happened—that his version is as real to him as hers is to her.

When Heidi is willing to stand in his shoes, Stuart will be relieved. He will see that she is not holding on fiercely to her version of the truth, but is willing to be wrong. He will be grateful that she wants to take the time to hear and understand him, and he will be well-disposed to working with her on a solution.

3. SHE CAN FIND HER PART IN THE SITUATION. "It takes two to tango," as the old saying goes. There are two people involved in any argument. That means each person is contributing to the situation at hand. Tempting as it may be to want to blame Stuart, Heidi will have to remind herself that she, too, has something to do with what's happening. That's not to say he didn't have a hand in it too—but focusing on him will lead to the same old ar-

guing. Instead, she can look for the ways she's been contributing to the situation and take responsibility for them. What in her history has been triggered? What assumptions is she making? What beliefs and expectations is she acting out? This is called *finding her part.* Once she finds her part, Heidi will be able to see what action she can take to remedy the dynamics between Stuart and herself. She can focus on the situation in a way that will bring a new freedom and a new result.

What does Heidi find when she looks for her part in the events of the past few weeks? She sees that she did a good job of effectively stating her needs and having Stuart agree to what she requested. The first time he called, though, instead of thanking him Heidi chastised him for not calling earlier. This hurt Stuart because in his eyes he was doing what she'd asked—yet she was adding on rules in the middle of the game. When she asked Stuart to call and let her know what he was doing, she hadn't specified how far ahead he should call.

Heidi can now see that her shortness on the phone felt like a rejection to Stuart. He was trying to do what she'd asked, and in her eyes he failed. Her apology made him feel better, and he was willing to continue complying with her request. So far, things were working okay. The next week he let her know ahead about the Nicks game, and even thought to call her when he knew he'd be home late. Once again, however, Heidi responded with anger when he called. This time Stuart's ego was bruised and he felt he'd been treated badly. He'd done what she'd asked him to do, and he was getting criticized again. Why even bother?

The following morning, Heidi's immediate attack gave Stuart little choice but to protect himself. He didn't think he'd done anything wrong, and now he had to defend himself. He decided that no matter what he did, she'd be angry—so he stopped trying. He withdrew and kept his defenses up. Every time Heidi tried to talk with him about why he was so withdrawn, he felt attacked and withdrew further. The situation was at an impasse.

Finding her part does not mean Heidi will start blaming herself for what's gone wrong. It means that she will review events in a matter-of-fact way and see that she contributed. She can see that she hadn't taken into account the effect she was having on Stuart. She hadn't been acknowledging him for doing what she'd asked of him. She'd been behaving as if she were responding to him and forgetting that he was also responding to her. She'd forgotten that her attitude mattered to him.

What would it be like for Heidi to own her part to Stuart? Let's look at how the scenario might go.

Heidi waits for a time when she and Stuart are relatively calm and when he's not occupied with something else. She places her hand on her heart. This allows her to connect to her love for Stuart, so she can speak from her heart.

Heidi says, "Stuart, this isn't easy for me to say, but I realize I made a mistake. I was hard on you when all you were trying to do was comply with my request. Then I attacked you rather than trying to have a calm, loving conversation. I'm so sorry."

Stuart looks at her, surprised. "You mean you're not mad at me anymore?"

"No," says Heidi. "I love you, and I can see that I was wrong."

"Oh, hon, it's okay," says Stuart. "I should have known not to call you in the middle of the night. I know how nervous you get when the phone rings late, thinking it's some disaster. I guess I just wasn't thinking."

Heidi reaches for Stuart, and they hug for a long time.

Once she found her part, Heidi was able to remind herself of her own power. Instead of feeling badly about herself, she was able to relax into knowing her own strength and trusting that there could be a solution. This allowed her to approach Stuart differently. Instead of accusing, she could open her heart to him. He responded positively to her compassion. In fact, all he really needed was acknowledgment. Once he felt heard, he could open his heart and acknowledge his own part.

OWNING YOUR PART

Owning your part is the most important thing you can do to nurture your relationship. In fact, in each of the stories we use as examples in the book, resolution comes when the woman owns her part in some way. It would be powerful for you to look for the point at which the woman owns her part in each story.

Owning your part is the opposite of blaming. When you blame, you give away your power. *When you own your part, you take your power back.* When you can look for your part in a situation and own what you've done to contribute in a matter-of-fact way, you are getting rid of the issue of blame. Instead of using your energy figuring out who started it, you can deal with the situation at hand in a loving, efficient manner.

﹏ *How to Own Your Part*

Put your hand on your heart. Remember a moment when you felt love for your man.

Write yourself the story of what happened in an objective way, stating only the *facts.* "I did this, he said that, I responded in this way," etc. Reread the story, making sure your story is made up of facts and not interpretations.

Look to your history to find the origin of the upset and attend to what needs healing.

Be willing to be wrong. You can be wrong *and* he can be wrong. They are not mutually exclusive!

Own your part. This does not mean blaming yourself. It means seeing your contribution and acknowledging it. That is all. And that is everything! When you own your part, he will be far more likely to own his. Then you can work on a solution together rather than pointing fingers at each other.

∾o∾

You are setting a generous example for your man by having an open heart, being willing to listen to him, being willing to see your part, being willing to stand in his shoes, and being willing to be wrong. Owning your part does not mean letting him off the hook for *his* part in it. Without a doubt, your man has done things that angered you and said things that hurt you. There is no question that it takes two to tango, and he has his part in it fair and square. Yet focusing on his part in it will keep you frustrated, angry, and resentful. When you are willing to be a generous example, you are an inspiration for him to follow your lead.

Your man is fortunate to be with someone like you—someone who is willing to examine how she contributes to a situation. Yet you're not doing it for him. You're doing it for *you*, so *you* can have a happy relationship. You're taking the lead and giving your man a loving approach to respond to.

ஜ The Power of Owning Your Part

YOU STOP FEELING LIKE YOUR RELATIONSHIP IS JUST HAPPENING TO YOU. If it's in your life, you have something to do with it. When you realize that, you get to stop feeling like a victim. And when you're no longer being the victim, you'll feel better and you can take positive action to change the situation.

SEEING YOUR CONTRIBUTION ALLOWS YOU TO SEE HOW POWERFUL YOU ARE. It may not always be the easiest thing to own your behaviors, words, moods, and thoughts that have added to the current situation. Sometimes it means looking at things you'd rather not see. When you're looking the other way, hoping for circumstances to change, you're giving away your power. Yet once you face yourself in this way, you are very powerful.

YOU HAVE THE OPPORTUNITY TO HEAL YOUR HISTORY. You can realize you've time-traveled and look to the past to see what you need to heal in order to have a good relationship. Why are you so upset? Who in your history are you being reminded of? What in your puzzle piece has you attracting this situation?

YOU CAN DROP THE FINGER OF BLAME AND START USING YOUR ENERGY IN A BETTER WAY. Seeing that your man is responding to you allows you to stop blaming him, and stopping the blame leaves you with a lot of extra time and energy on your hands. He'll be relieved when he feels the burden of blame lift, and he will feel much more inclined to do what will make you happy.

IT ALLOWS HIM TO MAKE YOU HAPPY. Your man wants you to be happy, but when you're right and he's wrong, you don't leave room for him to please you. When you drop the finger of blame, you can provide a generous example. Be willing to see his side—then *he* will be grateful and *you* can allow him to make you happy.

WHEN YOU'RE NOT BLAMING HIM, YOU CAN OPEN YOUR HEART TO HIM. It's impossible to be angry and have an open heart. It's impossible to hold a grudge and have an open heart. It's impossible to be critical and have an open heart. When your heart is open, you can have compassion for his confusion, hurt, anger, and vulnerability—and for your own. You can remember why you love him and state your needs from a caring place rather than an place of anger.

YOU CAN SEE THAT YOU ARE CAPABLE OF HURTING HIM BECAUSE HE IS VULNERABLE TO YOU. When you own how powerful you are in your relationship, you begin to understand how vulnerable your man is. He wants your love and approval, and instead he's getting a lot of your frustration and criticism. When he feels hurt, he closes off. Owning your part allows you to feel softer toward him. Feeling softer toward him attracts the love you want because it allows *him* to be softer...and that's what you want, isn't it?

IT ALLOWS YOU TO SEE WHAT YOU CAN DO TO CHANGE THE SITUATION. Don't like the way your relationship is going? Take charge by finding your part and doing what you can to shift your effect. You'll be amazed at how the situation can transform.

IT ALLOWS YOU TO BE CHERISHED. When Heidi owned her part with Stuart, they were able to open their hearts to each other. Instead of being defensive and blaming, Heidi created space to be cherished. Stuart was only too happy to fill that space. Your man wants to cherish you, and it's much easier when you're owning your part.

YOU BUILD A MUSCLE YOU CAN USE IN MANY OTHER CIRCUMSTANCES. Once you've learned how to own your part with your man, you can take that ability with you wherever you go. Owning your part is powerful in *any* arena—whether you're interacting with your boss, your coworkers, your parents, your children, your siblings, or your friends. You'll find yourself experiencing more satisfaction in all your relationships.

♡ ♡ ♡

Think of an issue you are currently having with your man.

Ask yourself the following questions:

> *Am I willing to own my part?*
>
> *What is my part?*
>
> *Am I willing to let him know?*
>
> *What is uncomfortable about letting him know?*
>
> *Am I willing to open my heart?*
>
> *What is uncomfortable about opening my heart?*
>
> *If I owned my part, what I'm afraid would happen is...*
>
> *If I owned my part, what would change is...*
>
> *Am I willing to be cherished?*

♡ ♡ ♡

CHAPTER SIX

OPENING YOUR HEART TO YOURSELF

LEARNING TO FORGIVE IS A CORNERSTONE of being cherished. It will make an enormous difference in your relationship. Why? Because the things you're holding against yourself, your man, and people from your past are all getting in the way of having the most loving, warm, cherishing relationship possible. If you're angry at your man or yourself, you may be thinking, "There are some things I can never forgive." That's okay—just read the chapters and the work will begin.

Veronica, a Life Works client, decided to throw a big party for her fortieth birthday. The only problem was that her boyfriend, Michael, hated large gatherings. In fact, he'd never been to one in the two years they'd been together. Yet Michael had been talking about marriage lately, and Veronica reasoned he'd have to learn to handle large groups if they were going to have a wedding. Also, he knew her fortieth was a milestone for her, and she was sure he'd realize how important it was to attend her party.

Still, Veronica hesitated when it came time to invite Michael. Even though he was working on it, she knew his issue with parties was very big. She mentioned the problem to her best friend, Tracy, who knew the situation.

"If he loves you, he'll come," Tracy said. The next morning Veronica took a deep breath, picked up the phone, and dialed Michael's number. "I have good news," she blurted. "I'm having a big bash for my fortieth birthday next month. I've invited everyone who's important to me and I can't wait for you to meet them. I just know you'll get along great with my family and you'll love my friends you haven't met and it will be the perfect occasion to meet everyone all at once, and it's going to be really fun, Tracy's helping me plan it."

"Hold on a second," said Michael. His voice sounded subdued. "You know how I am about parties. I hate to disappoint you but I don't think I'll be able to come. I'd really rather meet everyone one at a time, you know, like I met Tracy. It works a lot better for me that way."

Veronica felt tears rising behind her eyes. "Oh, Michael, I know crowds are a phobia of yours or whatever, but couldn't you try to overcome it just this once? Even for a little bit? This is really important to me."

Silence. Veronica counted to five and then said, "Michael?"

"I'm here," he said. "Look, if it's that important to you I will try to come."

"Promise?"

"I promise," said Michael.

A month later Veronica was standing on the patio at the Cactus Café, surveying her guests eating enchiladas and drinking margaritas. The band was swinging and everyone was having a good time. Only one thing was missing.

"Where's Michael?" Tracy hissed.

"He'll come," said Veronica. "I'll just call him to see what's holding him up." But he didn't answer his phone.

"He must be on his way," she hoped.

By ten, however, Veronica had to admit to herself that Michael wasn't coming. She told everyone he'd gotten food poisoning and hadn't been able to leave his house, smiling and assuring them he'd be all right. But she felt embarrassed. If Michael couldn't even come to her fortieth birthday party, how would they be able to have a wedding? Tracy was right—if he loved her, he would have come. Instead he had broken his promise and left her alone to field the curious questions of her guests.

The next morning Michael called her.

"Hi, Sunshine," he said. "Listen—I'm really, really sorry I couldn't make it to your party. I just couldn't do it. I got dressed up and drove all the way to the restaurant, but I couldn't make myself go in. I really tried, but I was sweating like crazy and it felt like I was having a heart attack. I just couldn't face being in a crowd with all those people. You understand, don't you? Please tell me you understand."

"Michael, you promised to come," said Veronica. "I told everyone you were going to be there and they were really excited to meet you. When you didn't show up I had to tell them you had food poisoning, but I'm sure everyone knew it was a lie."

"Why did you tell everyone I'd be there when you knew I might not be able to make it?" Michael asked.

"Because you *said* you would come," Veronica said. "You promised!"

"I promised to *try*, Veronica," Michael said. "Didn't the party go great anyway? Look, let's forget this whole thing. I'll make you dinner tonight."

Veronica felt a sob catch in her throat. "I can't, Michael," she said. "I'm so hurt, and I'll never be able to forgive you for not showing up."

"What are you saying?"

"Listen, if you can't make it to a party, how do you think you'd be able to go through with a wedding? It's never going to work, Michael."

"Are you breaking up with me?" Michael's voice cracked.

"Yes. I want to get married, and I don't want to spend any more time with someone who can't give me what I want." Veronica knew she sounded cruel, but she was afraid she'd give in if she wasn't firm. "I have too much self-respect to be with someone who would disappoint me like this."

"Well, I guess it's over then," said Michael despondently.

"I guess it is," agreed Veronica. She hung up quickly so he wouldn't hear her crying.

Veronica was sure she was right to break up with Michael, but the following weeks found her feeling increasingly awful. She missed Michael, and the party now didn't seem nearly as important to her as being with him. She found herself wondering if she'd be alone forever. Some days she felt so bad that she couldn't even get out of bed. Finally she sought help from a Life Works Guidess.

Veronica's Guidess helped her realize that her distress was twofold. She was angry at Michael, and she was also angry at herself. Her anger at Michael had faded with time, but her anger at herself for breaking up with him grew. How could she have been so mean to such a nice guy—one who had always treated her well? How could she ever forgive herself?

WHO'S TO BLAME?

Realizing you're holding something against yourself is the first step to being able to forgive yourself. And forgiveness is necessary because it opens your heart. We all have things we need to forgive ourselves for—and also things we need to forgive others for. We're often reluctant to forgive, however, because we think holding a grudge will protect us from getting hurt again. Being angry feels more powerful than being forgiving because it gives us the illusion of being in control. Yet in reality, to the extent that we are angry, resentful, and holding grudges, our hearts are closed off to love. When our hearts are closed, we can't let in the love that is all around us—and we also can't feel the love we have for others.

When Veronica realized how mad she was at herself for breaking up with Michael, she consulted her Life Works Guidess. She asked Veronica to look into her past for something she might need to forgive herself for. Veronica reluctantly mentioned a girl she had teased in third grade just because everyone else did—even though Veronica felt bad about it at the time.

How could Veronica's third-grade experience have anything to do with breaking up with Michael? Because, as she discovered, forgiving yourself begins with your history. We hold grudges against ourselves for things others often don't even recall. Some of the incidents are more dramatic, of course—the ones that make your hair stand on end or your stomach curdle when you think about them. Not everyone has big, dramatic incidents, though. Mostly, we need to forgive ourselves for the small things.

In order to open your heart and have the relationship you long for, you'll want to start forgiving yourself for things that happened in the past...even things that happened in childhood. In Veronica's case, it was important to remember, and forgive herself for, the girl she teased in elementary school. While working in a Guiding session, Veronica also noticed that after she ended her relationship with Michael, she was feeling the same way she'd felt at thirteen when she broke up with Patrick, her first boyfriend. At the time, her best friend had been teasing her about Patrick, saying he was a geek because he wore glasses and didn't like sports. Veronica gave in to peer pressure and ended it with Patrick in the school cafeteria. To her horror, he started to cry in front of everyone. Of course, Veronica was only in junior high, so she didn't know better—yet she'd felt bad for all those years about hurting Patrick. And, although it seemed ridiculous to admit it, she felt the same way about breaking up with Michael.

It's amazing how we tend to repeat the past until it is healed. What's the first step toward healing that past? It's not to find that third-grader you teased on the playground or to apologize to your junior high school boyfriend. The first thing to do is get back into a loving relationship with yourself. You can begin by asking yourself several times a day, "What's the most loving thing I can do for myself right now?" This will get you in touch with your heart and allow it to start opening to yourself again. Then when you're ready, you can release the old grudge you've been holding against yourself. Remember, that child, teenager, or woman you were in the past made mistakes, just as anybody else in the population would. Have compassion for her and forgive her for doing the best she could at the time. Once you forgive, you'll feel lighter—as if a burden has been lifted.

❦ ❦ ❦

Think of a time...

*You were in a situation and thought you were tak
ing care of yourself, then realized you weren't.*

*You thought you were doing something good and then
realized you were making a mistake.*

❦ ❦ ❦

FORGIVENESS IS...

Forgiveness is an experience of the heart, a release that creates
an opening for love. It is the key to opening your heart to yourself and your man so you can have a luscious, heartfelt relationship. Like Veronica, we all have things to forgive ourselves for.
Forgiving means releasing to the past what happened in the past
and letting go of old hurts, resentments, and grudges. Each thing
we haven't forgiven keeps our hearts closed a little more.

Why forgive? Because when you haven't forgiven, you are
dragging your history around with you into every relationship in
your life. It's a heavy load—and yet you're probably accustomed
to carrying it, so you might not have realized how much it weighs
you down, keeps other people away, and ends up hurting you. Not
forgiving ultimately harms you because you won't be able to feel
the love you have for others, and you won't be able to feel the love
others have for you.

Not forgiving can lead to resentment, anger, blame, guilt, and
mistrust. It can keep you repeating patterns from the past, pushing away intimacy, closing yourself off to new experiences, having painful relationships, and not trusting yourself to take care of
yourself.

You might not have realized how many grudges you're holding

against yourself from the past. Things you might be holding against yourself include:

> Breaking someone's heart
>
> Pushing someone away who cared about you
>
> Treating someone with disrespect
>
> Allowing yourself to be vulnerable so someone could hurt you
>
> Allowing yourself to be treated badly
>
> Doing something you wish you hadn't done
>
> Not doing something you wish you had done
>
> Saying something you wish you hadn't said
>
> Not saying something you wish you had said

Of course, it's natural to hold things against yourself. Why do we do it? Out of a natural instinct for self-protection. Holding on to guilt makes us feel as if we've learned a lesson. Not forgiving keeps us feeling safe because we can say to ourselves, "If I hold on to this, then it won't happen again." But you can keep yourself safe from something happening again and yet still forgive yourself. There are two steps to doing this—remembering what happened, and learning from your mistake.

First, remember that you have specific trouble spots. You have a tendency to make certain mistakes in relationship. Remember, too, that you're living in a trial-and-error universe. It is inevitable that you will make mistakes—it can't be avoided. Yet you don't have to keep making the *same* mistakes. Remembering keeps you awake to your trouble spots. Tell yourself you'll stay awake to them and notice them. When you remember, you're safe, because you know you don't have to do the same thing again. You can recall what happened last time and choose a different course of action.

Second, realize what you've learned. Your mistakes are where you can learn about what works and doesn't work. When you learn from them, you don't have to repeat them. Once you know you've learned the lesson, you can forgive yourself and move on. Then every experience ends up being a good one to have because it brings you to a better place. For example, Veronica realized she'd been having a conversation with herself that went like this:

"If I hold on to being angry at myself for breaking up with Patrick, then I won't let it happen again."

She saw that she could change that "if...then" conversation to a more supportive one that went like this:

"I have a pattern of leaving someone when I'm embarrassed—and then I hurt that person and feel terrible about it. If I stay awake and notice the next time that happens, I can keep myself from doing it again."

Knowing she had learned from what she did allowed Veronica to forgive herself. Once she saw that the reason for her upset was historical and had little to do with Michael, she discovered how badly she felt without him—and realized she really loved him. Since she was no longer holding her behavior against herself, she was finally able to call Michael and apologize.

"I'm sorry," she said when he picked up. And she felt her apology coming from her heart.

Michael forgave her. And when she knew she would remember her trouble spot and could count on herself not to leave him, or hurt him, the next time her pattern recurred, Veronica was able to forgive herself, too.

Forgiving will allow you to...

Release yourself from the ties of the past

Discover hidden motivations that might have been
holding you back

Love yourself more

Love others more

Be able to receive love from others

Accept that we are all human instead of struggling
against it

Be better able to relax and enjoy your life

Have more creative energy

Take life more lightly

Have heightened compassion

Know you can trust yourself to do what's good for you

Open your heart so you can have what you want with
your man

✍ How to Forgive

The following exercise will allow you to release grudges and let go of what's keeping your
heart closed off. To forgive, you'll want to go
through all the steps, even if you need to take a
break and return to it later. You will be glad you
did, because you will experience rewards in the
form of increased love and satisfaction in your
relationship—and in many facets of your life.

Using the following categories, ask yourself,
"What do I want to forgive myself for?"

With family

With friends

With colleagues

With myself

How I've treated myself

Things I've done that I wish I hadn't

Things I haven't done that I wish I had

For each answer, do the following exercise:

1. Hold your hand on your heart.

2. Remind yourself lovingly:

   This is a trial-and-error universe.

   I won't always get it right.

   It's not whether I'm going to have regrets, it's which regrets I'll have.

   This is one of them.

3. Compassionately see that you were doing the best you could then—rather than dwelling on what you would do now with the wisdom only hindsight can give you.

4. Remember why you made that decision. You had good reason for it then.

5. Think about what you can learn from this mistake or regret.

6. Are you willing to learn the lesson?

7. Think about what you want to remember from this experience.

a. Remember that certain people in your life will hurt you in certain ways, and not to expect them to be different next time. People do what they do. It's up to you to remember they do that.

b. Remember that this is something that you are particularly vulnerable to, probably because of something that happened in childhood. Remember to be awake to read the signs so you can see it coming.

8. Imagine a possible time in the future when you can use what you learned. Visualize yourself in that situation doing it differently because of what you've learned.

9. See if there is anything you can do about the issue you're working on now. If so, do it. If not...

10. Let it go. Release it to the past. Your heart will open when you do this. You will allow more love in and you will experience more love for others.

CHAPTER SEVEN

OPENING YOUR
HEART TO HIM

FLORENCE WALKED THROUGH HER FRONT DOOR with a sigh. It had been a long day at the hospital where she volunteered once a week. She hoped Neil had remembered to put in the lasagna as she'd asked him to that morning. She was famished.

"Neil?" she called, pulling off her gloves. She walked into the living room expecting to see him sitting near the window reading, as he usually was this time of the evening. But he wasn't there. Maybe he was in the kitchen, making a salad for dinner. That would be a delightful surprise.

Florence went into the kitchen, and sure enough, there was Neil. But he wasn't cooking. He was sitting at the table with the parts of a model airplane spread out all around him, humming to himself. Florence glanced at the lasagna sitting on the counter where she'd left it that morning, with a note taped to it giving Neil directions for how to heat it up.

"Neil," she said sharply. His head jerked up.

"Oh, hi, dear," he said. "I guess I was so involved with this airplane that I didn't hear you come in. I've been waiting for this model to come out for two years."

Florence sighed. "Neil, you forgot to put the lasagna in the oven."

"Oh, sorry," he said, casting a cursory glance at the counter. "Lost track of time."

Suddenly Florence felt exhausted. She was so tired of being the one who had to take care of the house, do the grocery shopping, make sure meals were prepared on time, do the laundry, and all the hundreds of other little chores she'd been doing for as long as she could remember. She'd thought it would be easier once the kids were out of the house, but since Dan, the youngest, had left for college last year nothing had changed. She was still the one who kept everything ticking and in apple-pie order. And she was sick of it. Suddenly she was sure she couldn't stand it one more minute.

"Neil, I am so sick and tired of being the one to do everything around here," Florence said. She dropped her keys on the counter and leaned against it, arms folded.

Neil put down the wing of the airplane he'd been carefully brushing glue onto.

"Why, Florence, it's not like you to complain," he said.

"Well, maybe it's about time I spoke up," Florence said. "I've had it. I've just had it. I thought that once the kids were all off at school and you'd dropped down to half-time at the plant, things would get a little easier for me around here. Like, maybe you'd lift a finger to help once in a while."

Neil just stared at her, astonished.

"Take the lasagna for example, Neil. *I* went out and bought the ingredients, for pete's sake. *I* cooked the darn thing and put it in the freezer on Sunday. *I* took it out this morning and *I* wrote a note with exact cooking directions for you so you could do the extremely simple job of putting it in the oven. But you couldn't even do that, could you? I'm gone all day visiting cancer patients, and you can't even have a hot supper that *I* prepared ready for me."

Florence burst into tears and ran from the room. She went into the bedroom, slammed the door, and threw herself across the bed, sobbing. A few minutes later, Neil knocked tentatively on the door.

"Florence, honey, are you okay?" he asked timidly.

"Go away!" Florence said. "I'm sick to death of you! I'm sick of meeting everyone else's needs when no one has a thought for mine!"

She heard Neil clear his throat and shift from foot to foot. The thought of him standing out there with a hangdog expression on his face made her feel more desperate.

"Neil, *go away!*" she yelled. She heard him shuffle off, and resumed sobbing. She felt an almost overwhelming discontent. Everything in her life seemed wrong. And Neil was no help. Did he care that she was having a hard time? No, he was out there in his La-Z-Boy watching TV like he always did. Falling back on the pillows, Florence decided she didn't want to see Neil right now. No, she would just stay here and let him sit out there with his television and his beer and wonder what she was doing. Maybe she would never go out there again. What did he really add to her life, anyway? After twenty-eight years of marriage, he still couldn't even put a lasagna in the oven.

Forgiving Your Man

Florence had been angry at Neil for years. Her resentment grew each time he failed to help with the dishes or forgot he'd promised to clean out the garage. With each grudge she compiled, her heart closed to him a little more. Now, she's reached a point of frustration that feels like there's no return. She's fed up with her life and it seems like it's all Neil's fault. So what can she do? She has a few choices.

She can continue being angry and resentful.

She can leave him.

She can forgive him.

Why should I be the one to forgive? Florence might wonder. He's the one who hasn't been pulling his weight all these years. Anyway, how could I possibly forgive him for all the years of disappointment?

Yet neither of the first two options are very tempting either. Florence is exhausted by being angry and is tired of feeling bad. She's ready for something to change, but she doesn't really want to leave. She still loves Neil, and they've built a life together. She doesn't want to be alone again after all this time.

The best way for Florence to get some relief is to choose the third option—forgiveness. She may resist it, yet it's what she will have to do if she wants to be happy and feel cherished. Forgiving Neil would be a loving thing to do for herself because it would allow her to release the anger that's been keeping her unhappy. She would feel lighter and there would be more space in her heart for love. She would be able to open her heart to Neil, and that would stimulate his heart to be open, too.

Like Florence, you may resist the idea of forgiving your man. After all, he has done things that hurt you, and you have good reason to be angry or resentful. There may be years of transgressions you've been holding against him, and you may have a long list of things he's done to humiliate or anger you. Yet in the end, holding on to that list ends up hurting *you*, not him. Why? Because it keeps you from being cherished. How can he cherish you when you're carrying around a list of his transgressions everywhere you go?

Believe it or not, your man is longing for you to open your heart to him. He yearns for your tenderness and compassion. He wants to be held in your heart as someone special and be treated with gentleness. He may not be able to tell you that's what he wants, and you may not be able to hear it even if he does tell you. You even have good reasons for keeping your heart closed to him. Yet at one time, you were open to him and gave him the love he craved. He chose to share his life with you because you made him feel special and cared for. He is yearning for you to open your heart to him again.

Since you've decided to stay with your man, then you will need to open your heart and forgive him. Not forgiving is too painful a way to live. If he's done things you are absolutely unwilling to forgive him for and you can't live with it...go! The in-between is purgatory, isn't it? It's only natural that you've closed off somewhat as you've been disappointed and hurt. You may have grown accustomed to closing the door on your man out of self-protection, because you've been hurt and you may be angry or disappointed. Yet now that you're becoming more aware, you've begun to see how softening and opening to him can be wonderful.

Imagine that your heart is a room with a door on it. You are in charge of opening and closing the door. Its hinges may be a bit rusty and reluctant to swing open, especially if things have been difficult with your man for a long time. Yet your heart-door is already more flexible since you've begun forgiving yourself. Forgiveness is the key to opening the door of your heart.

Like forgiving yourself, forgiving your man means releasing the past to the past. If there is something you can do to redress a past wrong today, by all means do it. Otherwise, letting it go is the healthiest thing to do. It takes much more energy to hold grudges and nurse resentments than it does to just let them float away, like letting go of a balloon and watching it disappear into the sky.

As we discussed in chapter 6, letting go may feel unsafe because you want to protect yourself from these hurtful things happening again. That's only natural. Yet the two steps of remembering and learning can allow you to be safe, and still forgive. In forgiving someone else, there are three steps that will allow you to forgive and still take care of yourself in the future.

✍ The Three Steps to Forgiving Someone Else

FIRST, as in chapter 6, *remember*. Remembering that people have hurt you in certain ways is essential for taking care of yourself. Maybe your man has forgotten to call at times when he said he would. Perhaps your sister never includes you in family discussions. Maybe your best friend always criticizes the presents your man gives you. There are things people have done to you that are definitely *not* okay. You have also done things that are not okay. But remembering will help you be prepared for the next time those things happen so that you can take care of yourself. Perhaps you can speak up so that those things won't happen again, or perhaps you'll respond to them differently. You can know that people always do certain things, and not take it personally.

THE SECOND STEP is to identify you have certain areas where you're particularly vulnerable to being hurt. Say you have a recurring sore spot about your man not calling frequently enough. Not forgiving him won't make him call more frequently! But remembering that you're vulnerable in this way will help you ask for what you need. You are awake to what can hurt you, and you forgive what has happened.

THIRD, learn the lesson. When you know that you have learned from what has happened in the past, you can forgive and move on.

∽⚭∾

✍ Warming Your Heart

To oil your hinges and make it easier to open your heart, ask yourself:

What am I holding against my man that I now see is in the way of our relationship working?

Write a list.

Then, do the following visualization to stimulate your forgiveness. Repeat it as often as you need to. Read through it first, then get comfortable, breathe deeply a few times, close your eyes, and play the visualization in your mind. You may want to place your hand over your heart to stimulate it with added energy.

Picture yourself in a dark movie theater. On the screen is the scene of a wonderful, loving event you experienced with your man. Whether you were sitting on a mountain peak together after a grueling hike, reading poetry while cuddling on the sofa, or sharing a bottle of champagne at a fancy restaurant, the feeling between you was warm, passionate, appreciative, and open. You were actively loving him and he was actively loving you. You felt the exchange of love and abandoned yourself to it.

Next, instead of sitting in the theater, allow yourself to become the woman in the movie. You are there with him in that loving moment, feeling his love bathing you and feeling your heart warm, soft, and open as you bathe him with your love in turn. You are appreciating him fully and caring for him as a complete human being. Now, notice the following and allow yourself to breathe into the experience of:

How you felt your love for him

Your desire for his well-being

Your appreciation for him and how he responded to your love

See that one of the reasons your man was so wonderful then was because of how you loved him, adored him, and treated him. Like a plant that gets the right amount of water, light, and nourishment from the soil to flourish, he flowered in your presence and showed the best of himself. Your care and attention brought it out. Your rose-colored glasses allowed him to see himself in the same flattering glow—and he reflected the glow back to you.

After allowing yourself to be fully in the wonderful experience of that loving moment, keep that warm feeling in your heart while you change the scene to a recent, present, or future situation that is difficult. Whether you argued in the car on the way to work this morning, you have an ongoing disagreement about where to go on vacation, or you're anticipating his resistance to your plans to visit your mother this weekend, place both of you in the situation.

Stay with the feelings of love and appreciation you felt in the past scenario. You can deepen your experience of it in the following ways:

Reflect on the fact that he had good psychological reasons for doing what he did.

See that he was not doing it to you, he was just doing what he does.

What do you need to learn from this situation to be safe in the future?

Are you willing to learn it?

What will you remember in order to protect yourself so that you can release the resentment from your heart?

Release the resentment and see it leaving your heart like a helium balloon floating out into the distance until it disappears.

Feel your heart as it opens. Breathe into the moment, letting the good feelings permeate your heart and your body. Slowly open your eyes, keeping the feelings of warmth and love in your heart.

If you are still very angry at your man after doing this visualization, allow yourself to remember how powerful you are. You have the power to allow your man to be more the way you want him to be. It may not happen right away, but when you shift your energy he will respond to you differently. Repeating this visualization often will allow your heart to further soften and open, and you will reap the benefits.

RELEASING OLD GRUDGES

It may be that, as Veronica discovered in chapter 6, some of the things you're angry about don't have anything to do with your man. It may seem like he's the one you're angry at, and he has certainly done things that have upset you. Yet it's likely the depth of your upset is partly historical. You are probably still carrying resentment from previous relationships. It would be worth your while to take a look at your history and see what you're upset about that may not have to do with the man you're with today. Then, you can do the following exercise to help you release old grudges. This will clear the path to forgiving your man in the present.

Releasing Past Relationships

I. Make a list of the men in your life who have been important to you, beginning as far back as you can remember. You might include your kindergarten crush, your boyfriend in junior high, and your first serious adult relationship.

2. Close your eyes and let the parade of men go past, one at a time. For each man, ask yourself:

What did I learn that was good from this relationship?

What did I learn about relationship from this man?

What did I learn about myself?

What did I learn to expect from men?

What did I learn about my being a woman?

With each man, see if anything is still unresolved.

3. Write a list of the things you think you need to let go of that you've been holding against men, so you can have the relationship you want now.

4. To release these old grudges refer to the 3 steps to forgiveness on page 130.

Oiling the Hinges

Forgiving your man means having compassion for the fact that he's human. You are two human beings having a relationship, and it's inevitable that you will hurt each other at times. In fact, that's what you are meant to be doing. Remember that people in relationship are like two rough stones bumping against each other to create two smooth stones. You *will* bump against each other—there is no way around it unless you simply avoid each other. If you never jostle each other, it means you don't get close. Having intimacy involves a certain amount of arguing and even hurting each other's feelings. That is part of having a close, loving relationship with a real human being on this planet.

When you forgive, you will feel lighter. There will be more space in your heart for love. You will notice that it's easier to swing open the doors to your heart—and when you have your heart open, it will stimulate his to be open. Having your heart open to your man is a practice, which means it might take some time to get good at it. It's like embarking on an exercise program. You don't start off running ten miles a day and lifting twenty-pound barbells, right? A sensible program that works means starting lightly and building up to a longer, more intense workout.

Your man is an important person to open your heart to, because he is the one you chose to share your life with. Yet opening your heart to him doesn't mean that you have to open it to others, or have it open in all situations. You are in charge of how open your heart is, who you open it to, and how long it's open, and with whom. In order to regulate your heart's openness, you will want to practice. Like building your biceps, your quadriceps, or any other muscle, it takes repetition and patience to develop the ability to open and close the door to your heart. The more you use the door to your heart, the more supple and willing the hinges will become. Doing the following exercise daily, or several times a day, will allow you to let love in with greater ease.

❧ *Heart Workout*

1. Close your eyes, breathe deeply a few times, and place your hand on your heart. Picture your heart as a room with a door that can be open any amount you like, a flower that can close up tightly or open completely to the sun, or any other opening/closing image that comes to you.

2. Notice how open or how closed your heart is at the moment.

3. Open your heart a little more. Notice how it feels to have it more open.

4. Open it further, then further, gradually opening it as far as you can.

5. Allow your heart to be open in a comfortable way that is appropriate at this moment.

6. Now imagine yourself in various stimulating circumstances with your man, such as talking about a challenging subject or being en route to visit a relative. Make a mental or written list of circumstances you find particularly stimulating. In each situation, notice how open your heart is and practice opening it further. Notice where it feels comfortable, where it feels uncomfortable, and why. Practice closing and opening your heart to different levels in each situation.

7. Say, "I can control how open my heart is in any situation."

Your relationship will work to the extent that you and your man have your hearts open to each other. When your heart becomes more elastic and its hinges smoother, you will notice that your relationship becomes deeper, richer, and more loving. In addition, oiling the hinges to your heart will benefit all your relationships—with family, friends, colleagues, and neighbors. Once you have a strong heart muscle, you can take it with you into any relationship or situation and enjoy greater freedom, love, and happiness.

Tips on having your heart open to him:

Be willing to be surprised.

Recognize that you are human.

Recognize that he is human.

Be willing to demonstrate your love.

Be willing to receive his demonstrations of love.

Be willing to be fascinated.

Remember that he is responding to you.

Be aware of the effect you have.

Know that you are doing it for you, so
you can be happier.

IT TAKES THE TIME IT TAKES

In chapter 6, learning to forgive allowed Veronica to open her heart to Michael. Releasing her anger was a relief. She recognized that a lot of her anger had to do with her history and didn't stem from Michael's actions. She no longer needed to hold on to her old grudges to feel safe. She realized that it felt far better to be able to forgive with an open heart than to hold on to her resentment. And Michael responded in kind, as if he'd been poised waiting for her to release her grudges and open her heart to him.

You, too, can open your heart to your man. It may take some time. Forgiveness may not happen all at once. It takes the time it takes. You can't release a grudge or regret until you are ready to release it. And you won't be ready to release it until you have opened your heart to yourself and him. The more you can open your heart, the more easily you will be able to accept that we are all human. You will have compassion for your own dilemma and for the dilemmas of others. You will assume that we are all doing the best we can and know we are living in a trial-and-error universe.

When you begin to forgive, your life will improve. You will know it is happening because you will be experiencing love more, both from yourself and from the people around you in your life. It's not that there will be more love, but you will be able to let in the love that is already all around you. The more you forgive, the more your heart will open. The more your heart opens, the more you will allow love in. When you have forgiven, you will have a deeper experience of love. You may find yourself getting teary more often over everyday occurrences because you will be letting them into your heart. You will be able to accept love in the way it is offered to you—even if it's awkward or doesn't fulfill your expectations. And you will be able to increasingly feel, both physically and emotionally, the love you have for others. You will experience love not as a concept or a thought, but as a real experience of the heart.

Do the "Warming Your Heart" visualization.

What do you need to support yourself in doing the visualization as many times as you need to?

What do you need to support you in doing the visualization when you need it?

Chapter Eight

Having More Intimacy

We all pay a lot of lip service to love. We say we want to be loved, that love is the most important thing, that love is all we need. Then, we do our best to push it away. It's true! Many of us find it hard to tolerate the love our men want to give us. Being loved is an intense experience. It's natural to be uncomfortable with it to some extent. The more we can forgive, and the more loving we can be toward ourselves, the more we can take in the love we want. To the extent that our hearts are closed, however, we will be pushing love away. There are a lot of ingenious ways of doing this. Ways we push love away include:

being busy

being critical

being cold

being distant

being curt

being sarcastic

pretending you don't care

being forgetful

being overworked

using the kids as an excuse or a barrier

worrying

complaining or nagging

not being pleasable

needing to be right all the time

laughing at his attempts to be close to you

fearing that he'll hurt you if you let him get too close

fearing that you'll hurt him if you get too close

feeling smothered

feeling dominated

fear of being trapped

shyness about sharing love, so you never return it

thinking you'll owe him too much

thinking now you'll have to give it back

not acknowledging that you're scared to be intimate

being afraid that you'll have to give up yourself in
order to be in a relationship

not feeling you deserve love

> not wanting to repeat your parents' relationship
>
> being unaccustomed to receiving love
>
> forgetting how good an open-hearted relationship feels

The love your man gives you may not look the way you expect it to or the way you think it should. Does he always want to hug you while you're cooking dinner? Does he get cuddly when you're tired? Does he try to fix things around the house when you'd rather call in a professional? Does he give you practical gifts when you'd prefer jewelry? Does he try to cheer you up when you just want to be alone and have a good cry?

It's likely that at least some of the time you end up annoyed by his expressions of affection. For instance, women tend to need to talk about their problems more than men do. Often all we need is to let someone know, and we don't necessarily want to be offered a solution. If you're going on about a problem and your man keeps wanting to fix it, it may be annoying to you. It seems like he's just trying to cut you off so he doesn't have to listen anymore. Yet his wanting to fix it probably means that he's doing what he would want *you* to do if *he* were having a problem.

If you're thinking, "All I want from a man is closeness," look again. The discomfort may be well hidden. When was the last time you really let your man express his love to you? When you open your heart and accept adoration you're vulnerable, and that can make you very uncomfortable. Part of your discomfort may come from subconscious vows you took in the past. For example, when someone broke up with you you decided "I'll never let anyone hurt me like that again." That vow would keep you from letting a man love you too much or get too close.

You may be unaware that you took vows, and you may not have realized that you're pushing love away. It's a way of protecting yourself—perhaps unconsciously. If you've had your heart broken, it's only natural that you would vow never to let it happen again. Heartbreak is painful, and no one wants to go through it over and over. Yet taking a vow never to let yourself get hurt like that again closes off your heart. You are no longer available to accept your man's love fully.

It is valuable for you to begin seeing the ways you've been pushing love away. Notice what level of intimacy or distance keeps you feeling comfortable. If you want more affection, you'll want to be aware of how you push your man's love away and look at the places that might need healing.

✍ *How to Stop Pushing Love Away*

Ask yourself, "Since when did I stop being satisfied with the love in my life?" When you find that moment, consider that your stuck spot.

Look for what happened just before the stuck spot. That is what needs healing.

Ask yourself, "What decisions or vows did I make then?" Let yourself be open for the answer to come.

Allow yourself to release the vows and mourn the original loss.

Stay awake and aware to how you're pushing love away.

You may have to look even further into your history than past relationships. Your tolerance for love—your ability to be intimate—was formed largely from your relationship with your parents. If you had an overly domineering or critical parent, it may not have felt safe to let them get too close. If you had a parent who smothered you, you may have decided too much love was overwhelming. If you had a distant parent, you might have closed yourself off from love in order to protect yourself from being disappointed. Knowing where your intimacy comfort zone originated can help you release your old patterns and open yourself to being loved.

It's amazing how many defenses we put up in order to keep love away, isn't it? Yet once you've identified how you have been keeping love at bay, you free yourself up to experience more of it. You'll be amazed to find how much love is already all around you. In fact, there is an unlimited abundance of love just waiting for you to open, warm, and soften your heart so you can receive it.

ভ ভ ভ

Did I have a parent who...

> *criticized?*
>
> *smothered?*
>
> *dominated?*
>
> *intruded?*
>
> *neglected?*
>
> *pushed me away?*

How have I been pushing my man's love away?

If I allowed myself to feel loved, what would be awkward is...

If I allowed love in, I would have to stop…

*If I allowed myself to be cherished, what would
change is…*
Do "How to stop pushing love away" exercise.

ॐ ॐ ॐ

RECEIVING LOVE

Your man is likely trying to give you a lot more love than you are receiving—or at least he did for some time. He may have given up by now. So why aren't you receiving all the love you desire? Your receiver, like most people's, may be in need of a tune-up. We tend to be raised in the belief that it's better to give than to receive. Yet when you're giving, you need someone to be receiving what it is you're offering. For a generous exchange, there needs to be a generous giver *and* a generous receiver.

Compliments are a good way to understand the importance of receiving. You've undoubtedly had the experience of giving a friend a heartfelt compliment, only to have her negate or deflect it. Didn't that take away from your enjoyment in giving it? By not receiving your compliment, she took away your opportunity to feel good about giving it. Receiving, then, is a generous act. If you give a friend a compliment and she receives it graciously, she is giving you a gift, too.

How good are you at receiving compliments? When your man tells you, "You look beautiful tonight," do you open your heart, take it in, and say, "Thank you"? Or do you immediately want to negate the compliment somehow, saying, "Oh, well, I couldn't get my hair to do exactly what I wanted," or, "Thanks, but I know the cleaner left some spots on this dress"? If you're like most of us, you probably have the immediate urge to downplay the compliment.

Receiving love is similar to receiving a compliment. In order to take it in, you have to have your heart open—not only to him, but to yourself. When you are loving yourself, you feel worthy of receiving love from someone else. When you are loving him, you are open to receiving the love he gives you in whatever way he gives it.

Receiving is powerful. It is generous of you to accept your man's expression of love—no matter what it looks like. This may mean biting your tongue when he gives you a sweater you hate, when he puts the dishes away in the wrong places, or when the surprise trip he's been planning turns out to be a fishing expedition or a sporting event. It would benefit you to be able to let go of your romantic ideal at times and see that he's doing his best to show you he loves you. If you really don't like it, you can receive it graciously and let him know gently at a later time how you *would* like it. "Honey, sometimes I really need to just discuss my feelings. It doesn't necessarily mean I want a solution, and I would love it if you could just sit and listen without offering advice."

It's generous of you to let your man know how to make you happy. That way, he doesn't have to fumble around trying to get it right and feel criticized when he doesn't. He can know exactly what you want, give it to you, and feel like a hero…and get you what you want.

Cultivating a Generous Heart

When you are receiving, your heart is open and your defenses are down—and this can feel uncomfortable. Since it's human nature to want to avoid uncomfortable feelings, we come up with lots of ways to avoid receiving the love coming our way. Things you may be doing to *not* receive include:

> Unknowingly starting an argument
>
> Holding grudges

Being fiercely independent

Closing down if you don't get the response
you want

Being uncommunicative

Criticizing him

Criticizing yourself

Changing the subject

Not letting him know what you want

Not being clear with yourself about what you
want

The thing about opening up to receiving is that it also opens us up to possible disappointment. And no one likes being disappointed, do they? Yet in order to be open to receiving good things, it's necessary to be willing to be disappointed. If you're unwilling to risk disappointment, it means you're also closed off to possibilities for joy and satisfaction. It is worth being willing to be disappointed. Disappointment, after all, is not lethal. The sadness of being disappointed may feel awful, yet it passes. The benefits of being open far outweigh the risks.

✒ How to Be a
Good Receiver

Being a good receiver, like opening your heart,
takes practice. We are all closed off to receiving
to some extent. In order to clear and expand your
ability to receive...

Practice taking compliments gracefully.

Practice receiving what your man offers you...even if it isn't exactly what you want.

Practice giving yourself good things.

Remind yourself that it's generous to be a good receiver.

Notice how you and others around you respond to being given to.

See your man's offerings as heartfelt attempts to make you happy.

Don't criticize his efforts.

Don't take things personally.

Don't turn disappointment into rejection.

Continue to expand your ability to take in love.

Learning to receive can bring you happiness you never dreamed of before. Your man wants to give to you and be your hero. Why not bask in the glow of his attention, receive what he offers, and know yourself to be loved? Be willing—accept what he offers, the way he offers it. Don't criticize or qualify his offering. A secret that works well is to accept something the way your man offers it five times. The next time, he'll be ready to listen to your feedback on how you'd *really* like it.

Receiving ability leaks out into other areas of your life, too. People want to give you presents, compliments, friendship, support, help...and when you are open to receiving them, you will be amazed at how much richer, happier, and more loving your life can be.

❦ ❦ ❦

Think of a time you were happily giving and the
recipient didn't receive your "gift" generously.
How did you feel?

Watch other people and their relationship to receiving.
What do you notice?

Observe how you push "gifts" away.

Are you willing to be a generous receiver?

What does your man offer you that you push away?
(If he's stopped giving, think back to when he
did give.)

Are you willing to receive what he has to offer even
if isn't exactly "right"?

Can you feel his interest in making you happy even
though he may not be "doing it right"?

❦ ❦ ❦

HOW TO LOVE HIM

Having your heart open to your man means being available to experience the warmth of your love for him. When you are experiencing love in your heart, there is less room for resentment, anger, or holding grudges. When you are feeling the love in your heart and letting it radiate outward, you are in a tender space where you can work things out calmly and lovingly with your man instead of accusing, criticizing, or blaming.

When you are coming from an openhearted stance, your man will reciprocate by having *his* heart open to *you*. When you go to him with true caring and compassion, he will be far more likely to approach you that way, too. If he doesn't do it at first, he will. He may not be used to your gentler approach and be defensive at first. After all, he's been longing to be known and understood by you for a while. When someone has an open heart, though, it is nearly impossible to be defensive or angry around them for long. He'll come around.

THE ASPECTS OF LOVE

"Love is a many-splendored thing." There are indeed many facets to love. In fact, love has six main aspects: compassion, forgiveness, gratefulness, generosity, the ability to be moved and inspired, and love itself. Focusing on and understanding the six aspects of love will begin to warm and open your heart further.

COMPASSION can be best summed up in the simple statement, "My heart is open to you." When your heart is open, you are able to experience the flow of love coming in and going out. You are not defended, wary, angry, resentful, or judgmental. You approach people and situations lovingly and with care.

Having compassion for your man means understanding that he is human, he will make mistakes, he's not a prince, and he's not perfect. Accepting that he is human means understanding that he has dilemmas and struggles of his own. Being human is difficult and complicated. He is just as confused, hurt, and caught up in the struggle as you are.

It is not always easy to accept that he's not exactly the way you want him to be, all of the time. Yet as you've come to understand more about his human nature, you have opened yourself up to accepting him as a whole, complete human being instead of someone who is there to make your life better.

Your man has very high expectations for how he's supposed to be. He often finds himself in a situation where he falls short of his own expectations, and it takes its toll. Being compassionate allows you to see that he's doing the best he can. If he could do better, he would. He usually knows or senses when he's messed up, and he doesn't need your disapproval heaped on his own feelings of inadequacy. He is not your enemy.

"My heart is open to you" is a simple phrase, yet it is very powerful. It's impossible to be angry, resentful, or critical *and* have your heart open. The minute your heart is open to your man, you are better able to put yourself in his shoes and understand his dilemma. You are able to accept him more fully for who he is, and be open to loving him nonjudgmentally from where you are standing. Opening your heart doesn't involve effort. There is nothing to do but breathe into your heart and feel it opening to the man with whom you chose to share your life.

FORGIVENESS is a heart-expanding process that you've already begun. You have become willing to let go of grudges you're holding against yourself, as well as understanding that people mess up—it's unavoidable. Now you can open your heart by forgiving your man. He has said or done things that hurt you, just as you have said or done things that hurt him. Whether they are major transgressions or minor annoyances, the things that haven't been forgiven clutter up your relationship. They become fuel for the fire when you get into an argument, inflaming anger out of proportion to the present circumstance.

Part of loving someone is being willing to forgive them their transgressions, slipups, and mistakes. When you are hurt by something your man has done, it's easy to forget that he is on your side. He starts to look like the enemy. It's natural to want to defend yourself by closing off your heart and becoming an impenetrable fortress. The irony is that when you hold on to anger and resentment, you become your *own* enemy. Closing off your heart damages you in the long run because when your heart is closed, you not only can't let love out, you can't take it in either.

Remembering that your man is on your side allows you to forgive him. When he makes a mistake, it doesn't mean he doesn't love you. It just means he made a mistake. He loves you *and* he's late. He loves you *and* he forgot. He loves you *and* he didn't do it the way you asked him to. He is doing the best he can—just as you are. You make mistakes, too, and you would like him to forgive you for them, wouldn't you? It's awful to stand in front of someone knowing they're holding against you something you did yesterday, last year, or ten years ago.

As we discussed in chapter 7, forgiving your man doesn't mean it's okay that he hurt you. It's never okay when someone hurts you. Yet holding on to a grudge hurts you more. Forgiveness means putting the past in the past. When you are no longer holding on to past hurts, you become lighter, freer, and more able to give and receive love.

GRATEFULNESS is a daily practice of remembering why you love your man and why you wanted him in your life. After all, he's the same man you fell in love with and decided to share your life with. It gets easy to lose sight of that in the everyday shuffle of life. Remembering that you love him, why you love him, and being thankful that he's here will warm your heart.

It is good to be aware of these three aspects of gratefulness:

> gratitude for who he is and what he does
>
> gratitude for what you work hard for together
>
> gratitude for what hasn't come yet but that is on its way to you

Your man adds texture to your daily life. If it seems like he hasn't for a long time, think back and remember what he did in the past. He still has it in him. It is good to be grateful for the qualities he brings. There are things he does that you may not even notice. It would be good to begin noticing those everyday things you may not even have named. Notice too that you have things to learn from him, and allow yourself to be grateful for them.

Gratefulness means noticing the little things he does every day that make your life more enjoyable—and thanking him for them. Does he make coffee for you in the morning or offer to change the oil in your car? Does he give you solutions to problems—even when you don't want to hear them? It can be all too easy to take his presence and his contribution for granted. It's powerful to honor and acknowledge what he does for you that you'd been praying a man would do for you.

Your man is beginning to shift in response to the shifts you're making as you read this book. Be open to feeling grateful to him for his shifts, for his willingness to love you and support you. Sometimes your man has a lot to deal with while he's loving you. He puts up with your mood swings, your worrying, your annoying habits…and he loves you anyway. It would be good to be grateful for that, and to let him know how much you appreciate his understanding. In return, he will appreciate your acknowledgment—and your hearts will be warmed toward each other.

GENEROSITY means giving without thinking of the return. Being generous means giving for the pure joy and pleasure of it. When you are generous with your man, you are giving him the benefit of the doubt. It's generous to assume that he's doing the best he can, and if he's not doing it the way you want, perhaps it's because he doesn't know how. It's generous of you to make it easier for him by telling him how you'd like it to be. When you withhold your desires, he doesn't know what to do and is likely to get it wrong. When he gives you something, it's generous of you to receive it gracefully. He wants to please you, remember?

It's generous to give him what he asks for, as long as it's healthy for you. Because he is less complicated than you, often what he asks is relatively easy for you to grant. It's generous of you to be pleasable. That means being a generous receiver—accepting what he offers you, the way he offers it. Extending your generosity to him provides inspiration for him to do the same. When you create romance, laughter, fun, lightness…that's what he will give back to you. It is generous to you and to him when you give freely of yourself. Your relationship benefits and you're both happier.

THE ABILITY TO BE MOVED AND INSPIRED is what we experience when witnessing people struggling, stretching, achieving against the odds, falling, and getting up again. There's dignity in the process. It's not perfection that moves us, but being human. We are inspired by watching someone try something he or she has never tried before, even if it looks clumsy. Think of watching a child's first attempts to hold a spoon or to stand. It's breathtaking, isn't it?

You were moved and inspired by your man at the beginning of your relationship, weren't you? That's what allowed you to let him into your life. He touched a chord in you, and you responded to it. When you fell in love with him, you felt more alive. He sparked something in you. In his presence, you were inspired to be the best person you could be.

It may be a long time since you felt moved and inspired by your man. Yet he's still the same man he was. Today, it would be good to be open to being moved and inspired by him again—by his struggles, his willingness to work through things with you, his vulnerability, and his ability to get through what's difficult. You may wish he were perfect, yet if he were, he wouldn't be able to spark that feeling of aliveness in you. It is his humanity that can move you to tears or inspire your creativity. Remember that your man is vulnerable...yet he is hanging in there, doing his best, and loving you through it. That's inspiring!

LOVE ITSELF is something we tend to think of abstractly, as a concept. So what does it mean to really love someone in a concrete sense? Loving your man means being on his side, gently helping him have what he wants that's good for him. It means being happy when he's happy, being careful when he's hurt, and being tender when things aren't working well for him. It means holding his hand when he needs comforting, and allowing him to hold yours when you need comforting. It means accepting him, trying to understand him, listening to him, giving him acknowledgment, and receiving the love he gives you.

Loving your man doesn't mean helping him have what

he wants that's *not* good for him, and it doesn't mean helping him have what's good for him that he *doesn't* want. It's a loving act to make sure he can get out to play golf once in a while if he loves it, but it's not loving to bake him brownies when he's trying to lose weight. When you are loving him, you're on the same team, working with him to be as happy and fulfilled as you both can be. When you are loving him, you are helping him be happily himself. You are wanting for him what he wants for himself. And he will do the same for you.

❦ ❦ ❦

What do you have to be compassionate about with him?

What do you have to be forgiving about?

What are you grateful to him for?

What can you give him generously that you may have been withholding?

What can you receive from him generously that you have previously rejected?

What in him moves and inspires you?

How can you gently support him in having what he wants that's good for him?

Every day, notice one thing he does for which you're grateful.

❦ ❦ ❦

CHAPTER NINE

BECOMING
IRRESISTIBLE

AT THE RECENT WEDDING OF A Life Works Guidess, two other Guidesses in attendance were touched by their husbands' chanting of "Happy wife, happy life. Happy wife, happy life." Some of the other guests joined in the chant, recognizing the truth of this singsong wisdom.

Believe it or not, we know the following is true: your happiness is the biggest factor for the success of your relationship. We may expect that we need to fix something about ourselves—usually on the outside—but men everywhere know that the key to a happy life is a happy woman. And they often don't know what to do to make you happy. In fact, the only person who can guarantee your happiness is *you*. That's why the most important relationship you have is with yourself. When you are loving yourself, you are open and available to be loved by others—and that makes you irresistible.

Loving yourself means:

> forgiving yourself for making mistakes
>
> forgiving yourself for letting things happen to you
>
> knowing you are doing the best you can
>
> knowing you are lovable
>
> taking a stand for yourself
>
> trusting that you will make good choices
>
> having your own life
>
> drawing toward you what you want
>
> being grateful for what comes to you
>
> looking to the future with optimism
>
> asking for and receiving support when you need it
>
> giving yourself the benefit of the doubt
>
> wanting what is good for you
>
> turning your back on what's not good for you
>
> letting things take the time they take
>
> knowing you are powerful

Being self-loving is not the same as being self-serving, self-centered, or selfish. Self-love is generous because when you are in love with yourself, you share your happiness and satisfaction with everyone in your life. If you are being a martyr, a victim, a nag, or a critic, you are not only being hard on yourself, but on everyone around you. And your relationship suffers. Remember that when you are happier, he's happier. He *wants* you to be happy, strong, centered, have your own life, and take care of yourself.

It's generous of you to spend time and energy on your relationship with yourself because when you're feeling nourished, nurtured, and loved, you will spread your happiness to your man. It's a circular process. When you are patient, loving, accepting, and compassionate with yourself, you will be that way with your man, too. He will respond in kind and you will experience more love from him. Then, you will want to open your heart to him even more. It's a win-win situation for both of you, and for all those around you.

When you are being self-loving in relationship, you are:

> doing things that are important to you that don't involve your man
>
> maintaining your own friendships
>
> taking care of your needs
>
> gently letting him know what will make you happy
>
> standing up for yourself when you need to
>
> giving yourself what you want that's good for you
>
> assuming you will be treated well and have what you want
>
> not taking things personally
>
> accepting that you're human and not perfect (yes, it's true!)
>
> having fun
>
> being pleasable
>
> enjoying your life

Think about it—how fun is it to be around someone who is constantly putting herself down, always on the defensive, being a doormat, or generally not enjoying her own life? How attracted are you to someone who must have it her way, anticipates being wronged, looks at life pessimistically, feels like a victim, is clingy, and is never satisfied? Not very.

You know how irresistible it is when an infant or toddler does something new, then crows with delight at her own ingenuity? That's a pure, unself-conscious enjoyment of herself stemming from self-love. Then that toddler grows up and learns to criticize herself. Her self-love becomes adulterated with doubt, fear, anger, feelings of unworthiness, and all the other scars life leaves on her. She no longer enjoys herself with the purity and unself-consciousness she had when she was two.

Being around someone who loves herself, is confident, has a good sense of humor, gently stands up for what she wants, and shares her love with others is a joy. When you are loving yourself well, you will be nurturing the parts of you that want to be expressed. You will be happier, your man will be happier, and your relationship will be better.

When you love yourself you're irresistible.

🐗 🐗 🐗

In what ways are you nurturing your relationship with yourself?

What more can you do to develop and nurture that relationship with yourself?

🐗 🐗 🐗

TAKING CARE OF YOURSELF

Before getting engaged, Danielle and Morris had been dating for three years, during which time they saw each other two or three times a week. Meanwhile, Danielle kept up a busy schedule that included weekly get-togethers with her friends, yoga classes, and frequent cultural outings to museums or concerts. She also set aside one night during the week to be alone, which gave her time to write in her journal, read the accumulated newspapers, and take a long bath. Doing the activities she loved kept her feeling connected to herself and excited about life. Morris was attracted to her independence and the radiance of a woman who was taking good care of her life on every level.

When Morris asked her to marry him, Danielle was thrilled. She immediately threw herself into planning her dream wedding and looking for houses. This kept her even busier than usual, so she stopped going to her yoga classes, and her cultural outings went by the wayside. By the weekend she was usually exhausted and begged off her get-togethers with friends. The nights she'd been accustomed to spending alone were now taken up with house-hunting or picking out invitations.

After the honeymoon, Danielle was still very busy as she worked on getting their new household in order. A few months later, she discovered she was pregnant. Now her time was filled with baby preparations. After her daughter, Debbie, was born, Danielle focused her life around her. She loved being a mother and was grateful that Morris made enough money for her to stay home with their daughter.

After a few months, though, Danielle found herself feeling curiously empty and dissatisfied. She began to notice that Morris worked late most nights during the week, and that on the weekends he generally spent Saturday golfing with his buddies. Sundays, he was too tired to do much except putter around the house. She was alone with the baby most of the time, and she began to chafe.

"I'm not happy," Danielle complained finally.

"What do you mean?" Morris asked, looking alarmed.

"Well, all I do is take care of the baby. I don't have any time to myself, and you and I don't spend time together the way we used to."

"But we have a family now. Doesn't that make you happy?"

"Yes, it does. In general I'm very content. But I'm exhausted and I haven't been taking care of myself very well. If you think about it, your life hasn't changed all that much. You still go to work and hang out with your buddies. My life, on the other hand, has changed drastically."

"Aren't you happy to be able to stay home and take care of Debbie? I thought you wanted to do that."

"I do, that's not what I'm saying. It's just that I think I need some time to myself so I can rejuvenate, and I would like us to have date nights once in a while."

Danielle's dilemma is a common one for women. When we get involved with a man or start a family, we often tend to give up doing the things that feed our souls and keep us feeling happy. It's no wonder we do this—we are trained from childhood to think our happiness will come when we find the right man, even if our mothers told us otherwise. We tend to focus on our family, making it the center of our lives. There is nothing inherently wrong with this, but the problem comes when we stop giving ourselves what *we* need in order to feel nourished.

What we may not have understood is that in general, men *want* their women to nurture themselves and love themselves. They want us to be happy, and they don't want to carry the responsibility for our happiness. It's a burden to be the center of someone else's life.

After talking with Morris, Danielle knew she needed to start doing the activities that fed her soul again. Her friend Amanda agreed to watch Debbie twice a week so Danielle could get to her yoga class, and Morris agreed to come home early every Friday and watch Debbie so Danielle could spend some time with her girlfriends.

Danielle felt excited and couldn't wait for her first yoga class. When it came time to leave Debbie with Amanda, however, she balked.

I've never left her before, Danielle mused in the car, feeling as if she were going to cry. I know I need to take care of myself, but this feels awful. Maybe I was wrong and I don't need time to myself.

As soon as Danielle walked into the yoga studio, though, she knew she was doing the right thing. She took a deep breath, realizing it had been months since she'd even thought about breathing. Sitting in lotus position, she let her mind relax.

Ah, she thought, it's worth a little discomfort at leaving Debbie to have this feeling of peace be able to drift through me.

If Danielle hadn't been aware that she had adjustments to make, she may have been tempted to make her relationship the problem. This is a common mistake many of us make. When we feel discontented, we put the responsibility on the man. "Since he's supposed to make me happy and I'm not happy, there must be something wrong with him." What we don't realize when we do this is that we have something to do with our own happiness. If we continue with, or discover, activities that nourish and revitalize us, we can take responsibility for our own happiness.

When Danielle took her happiness into her own hands, she discovered that:

1. She felt nurtured because she was taking care of herself.

2. Doing the activities she loved and spending

time alone refreshed and rejuvenated her.

3. Morris was thrilled with her new, energetic attitude.

4. She could look at Morris as a partner rather than an adversary.

5. She was happy with herself, her relationship, and her new family.

Since how good or bad your relationship is depends so much on your happiness, it follows that if you want your relationship to be better, the place to work on it is in yourself. If things are going to change in your relationship, it is because *you* change. You can't do much about how he is, no matter how badly you want to. *Your place of power is in yourself.* You are the one who can make the shifts needed for your relationship to flourish.

Being Pleasable

"Mom, are you sitting down?" Lydia asked, twirling her curly hair around a finger.

"No, should I be?" Her mother's voice was eager.

Lydia couldn't contain her excitement any longer. "Mom, Eric asked me to marry him!"

"Oh, my," her mother breathed. "I'm sitting down row. Oh, honey, congratulations! Tell me all about it. Did he get down on one knee? What's the ring like?"

"Well..." Lydia hesitated. "There isn't a ring yet. We've actually been looking at rings for a while, but we can't seem to agree on one."

"What do you mean?" her mother asked.

"Well, Eric can't see why it's so important to me to have a vintage ring. You know how I love the colors in older diamonds. And when I explained to him how diamonds today are selected for purity and not for color, he thought I was nuts. There's this gorgeous two-carat nineteen-thirties diamond I want; it's the perfect shape and size and just radiates the colors of the rainbow, but Eric thinks it's too expensive and a little flashy..."

"Honey, you deserve to have what you want," Lydia's mother said. "The ring is for you, not for him. He may not understand why it's so important to you—men rarely do. But he wants you to be happy, trust me. So be gentle but firm. You deserve the ring that makes you happy."

Lydia took her mother's advice and explained to Eric yet again how important the vintage ring was to her. Finally he saw her viewpoint, of course, and wanted her to be happy. He slipped the ring into her coat pocket one day when she wasn't looking. When she reached into the pocket for her keys, Lydia shrieked for joy and threw her arms around Eric.

"Honey, you've made me so happy," she whispered into his ear. "Not only do I have the best man in the world, I have the most beautiful ring." Eric grunted, pretending surliness, but he couldn't stop the smile from spreading over his face.

That evening Lydia and Eric joined some friends for dinner, and Lydia couldn't contain her excitement as she flashed her ring around for them all to ooh and aah over. As she babbled excitedly with the women in the group, she noticed Eric talking seriously with the men about how he'd managed to find the exact ring she wanted. He put his arm around her proudly and took her hand, pointing out how the diamond was cut to sparkle in all the colors of the rainbow. Lydia smiled inwardly, remembering her mother's advice.

"Thanks, Mom," she said to herself. "You were right—Eric just wants me to be happy, and then he feels like a million bucks, too!"

Like Lydia, many of us have to help their men see why it's important to have what we want. Like Eric, many men don't see what the big deal is and they resist the whole process. But once he is able to help her have what she wants, you can bet he is swelling with pride.

This holds true in almost every area of life, not just with material gifts. Whether he has figured out how to fix the computer, gotten a promotion, planted a tree, or chosen a great restaurant for dinner, a man wants your acknowledgment. It makes him feel good when you enjoy what he gives you. It feeds his ego to know that he can make you happy. To put it simply, your man wants you to feel good in his presence for two reasons:

1. He knows his life is easier when you are happy.

2. When you feel good in his presence, he feels like a hero.

It's not always easy to make you happy. Since you are more subject to moods and emotions than he is, you may tend to be harder to please. It may often seem that he's holding back from expressing his emotions, and this can be annoying. Yet in reality, he is often looking to you for emotional clues. He is not as complex as you are, and he is easier to please. In fact, for that reason he probably enjoys the relationship more than you do. And his ability to enjoy it is directly proportional to your happiness. That's why it's important for you to be pleasable.

Lydia let Eric know gently and clearly that she wanted the vintage ring. Since Eric wanted to make her happy, he got it for her even though he had reservations. Then, Lydia allowed herself to be pleased—and let him know it. When Lydia was thrilled with "his" choice of an engagement ring, Eric felt proud of himself. He was happy to display the ring to his friends, knowing he'd made his new fiancée the gift of a lifetime. He loved seeing how happily Lydia flashed the ring around, telling everyone about it. He felt like a hero—and Lydia had what she wanted.

When you are unhappy, it's likely that your man gets the brunt of your dissatisfaction—if only because he's the one who is directly in your line of fire. When you're communicating your unhappiness to him, he takes it personally. If he doesn't know how to fix the situation, he begins to feel like a failure. If Lydia had hoped Eric would read her mind instead of being clear about her desire, she could have ended up with a ring she didn't want. She may have become resentful, feeling that Eric didn't value her enough to give her the ring of her dreams. Her resentment may have filtered into other aspects of her engagement—and who knows what mischief she could have caused? Being clear, calm, loving, and communicative about what she wanted created a happy scenario for both of them.

Sometimes no matter how clear you may be, your man still gives you a gift you don't like or expresses his love in a way that makes you uncomfortable. Yet since he's doing it with the best intentions, he'll be hurt and humiliated if you criticize his efforts. If he brings you coffee with sugar when you like it black, accept it graciously. Isn't it great that you have a man in your life to bring you coffee? Once, you would have given anything for a man to share the intimate details of your life. Being grateful he's there will allow you to be pleasable. When you are happy and let your man know he is contributing to your happiness, he feels like a success. He is your hero—and he will do anything for you.

You're Irresistible When...

You are irresistible when you are knowing and accepting yourself, nurturing yourself, being tender with yourself, taking time to do the things that are important to you, having a life, and treating yourself with loving care. When you are doing these things, you are powerful. That doesn't mean you're lording it over your man or trying to force things to be different. It means you're experiencing the fullness of your self and expressing it naturally. And when you're doing that, you are living life fully and joyfully.

You are irresistible to your man when...

> You are being yourself and enjoying it.
>
> You are happy.
>
> You are really listening to him.
>
> You are understanding him.
>
> You are accepting him.
>
> You are allowing him to please you.
>
> You are having fun.
>
> You praise him for his efforts.
>
> You feel attractive.
>
> You let him know how attractive you find him.
>
> You let him feel like a hero.
>
> You let him know how much you love him.
>
> You have your heart open to him.

❦ ❦ ❦

*Think of a time when your unhappiness influenced your
     relationship.*
What could you have done to help yourself?
*Think of a time when your happiness influenced
     your relationship.*
What happened for him? What happened between you?
How does your man show you he wants you to be happy?
(Look closely—his style may be subtle).
In the next few weeks...
*1. Observe how he is when you are happy.
     What does he do?*

*2. Observe how he is when you are unhappy.
     How does he act?*

❦ ❦ ❦

Chapter Ten

Stepping into His Shoes

MINDY AND WILL LOVED EACH OTHER PASSIONATELY, and they also fought passionately. Whether the fight was about what kind of bread to have with spaghetti or which set of parents to visit for the holidays, Mindy and Will each took a side and stuck to it no matter what. For years, they agreed that their fierceness added excitement to their relationship. Eventually, though, the arguing escalated and began to take its toll. One day, exhausted after a three-hour argument about Mindy's sister, Jill, they agreed it was time to get help for their relationship.

A few days later, Mindy and Will met at Life Works on their lunch hour. Seated on the sofa across from Carol, the Guidess Mindy had chosen to help them, they looked at each other nervously.

"So tell me a little about why you're here," Carol said.

Mindy took a deep breath. "We're here because we fight a lot. We've always argued and enjoyed it as part of our dynamic partnership, but lately it seems like our arguments have been getting nastier and take more out of us. We just can't agree on things, and it drives us crazy. Well, it drives me crazy anyway."

Carol looked at Will.

"Mindy pretty much summed it up," Will said. "I guess we've always agreed to disagree because we're both opinionated and kind of stubborn. In the past couple of years, though, it seems like we're not respecting that agreement, if you know what I mean. We just rip each other apart when we argue, and I for one am really sick of it."

"When was the last time you argued?" Carol asked.

"Last night," they chorused.

Mindy giggled nervously. "Well, at least we agree on that."

Carol smiled. "I'd like to get a feel for how your arguments go, so let's use last night's argument as a sample. Will, why don't you give me your version while Mindy just listens. Then, Mindy, you can give me your version."

Will put the tips of his fingers together, frowning in concentration. "Okay, umm, it started when Mindy mentioned a letter she'd gotten from her younger sister Jill about Jill's daughter Nicole. Every time Mindy hears from Jill, she gets really defensive and assumes I'm not going to listen to her, I guess. So she said, 'Jill wants us to sign some kind of paper naming us as Nicole's guardian in case something happens to Jill. I'm signing it and I hope you do, too.'

"It was like Mindy had already decided what we were going to do before consulting me, so naturally I got a little upset. I tried to stay calm and asked her if she'd taken into consideration all the legal angles and the responsibility it would entail. Not to mention the custody battles we could get into if Nicole's father ever decided to show up on the scene again. He left Jill before Nicole was born and disappeared, but you never know. Anyway, I was trying to be the voice of reason as usual, and Mindy just started ranting at me about how I hate her sister, how unfairly I treat her, and how I never give her sister credit for anything."

"How did you respond to her?" Carol asked.

"I couldn't really get a word in edgewise, but I tried to tell Mindy that this had nothing to do with her sister—that I was just trying to look at all the angles before we made a decision. Also that it wasn't fair of her to present it to me as already decided when she hadn't even asked me about it yet. But my defense fell on deaf ears, I'm afraid. Finally I gave up and went into my study for some peace and quiet."

Mindy leaned forward urgently. "He's distorting the truth like he always does, to make him sound like the reasonable one and me sound like an emotional, out-of-control freak! I did not say I'd already signed the document. I said I'd *like* to sign it. There's a big difference there. And if I was a little defensive, it's because Will always jumps down my throat about wanting to help my sister. She's only twenty-four, for goodness' sake, and she doesn't get any help from my parents. If he'd only be a little more understanding and less black and white…"

"Try to stick to what happened last night," Carol said softly.

"Okay, last night. Hmm. I guess I did get upset, because I felt like Will was already rejecting the idea of being Nicole's guardian just because it had to do with my sister. He started firing questions at me and not waiting for my answers. Finally I had to yell to try and get his attention, and then he stormed off into his study and slammed the door."

Mindy sat back with a flounce and glared at Will. He glared back at her. Then they both turned to Carol as she said, "Let's use that argument as a jumping-off place. It gives us a lot of food for thought and a good place to begin our work. From what I'm hearing, it sounds like you two are not really so far apart in your views, yet you have trouble communicating them to each other calmly and lovingly. That's something we can work on. It's important for you to learn how to communicate without making assumptions and judging each other."

WALKING A MILE IN HIS SHOES

An old adage says that you don't really know a man until you've walked a mile in his footwear. In the above scenario, it's clear that Mindy has not walked a mile in Will's loafers—even though she loves him and has been in relationship with him for twelve years. Why is she so reluctant to step into his shoes and see his reality? Because she's certain her version of reality is the only one—as is Will.

In some ways, you have probably been just as wedded to your version of reality as Mindy is. It doesn't help that your man may not be willing to see your version of the truth either. In fact, you may not even have considered stepping into your man's shoes because you're busy trying to convince him that you're right. It can be really hard to understand how he can see things so differently than you do. You might even think he's twisting the truth to fit his own agenda. But unless you're with a pathological liar, which is unlikely, chances are your man is just experiencing things differently than you do.

What is important to understand is that your perception depends on where you are standing. A room looks different if you're standing in the doorway than it does when you're in the corner. Your perception of what's happening between you and your man is different from his. Not only are you standing in different shoes, but you bring all your past experiences into the present circumstance. Your history follows you everywhere, and his follows him. Naturally, you will not perceive the same experience in exactly the same way.

Since perception depends on personal history and interpretation, it means there is no right way and no wrong way to interpret an event, an object, or a discussion. This may be hard to swallow—because women like to be right, don't we? Yet accepting that his viewpoint is as valid as yours is an essential ingredient in having a loving, understanding give-and-take in your relationship.

Mindy discovered just how rewarding it could be to let go of being right and be willing to see things from Will's viewpoint. After a few weeks of Guiding, in fact, she was shocked to realize that she was learning things about Will she had never known before. In the process she was gaining a new respect for him. Instead of hearing that he was just trying to make things difficult, she now saw that Will gave important issues serious consideration. In fact, he was able to see things with an objective overall viewpoint that Mindy didn't always have.

"We've been together for twelve years, and I don't know if I've ever really *seen* him or *heard* him," she marveled to Carol.

"Isn't it amazing what can happen when you really start listening to him and trying to understand him?" Carol said. "Women tend to make men into objects instead of really seeing and accepting them as individual human beings. We get really busy comparing them to how we think they should be or what function they should be fulfilling in our lives, and we forget that they're separate and different."

"It feels great when Mindy listens to me and doesn't finish my sentences for me," Will put in. "It was so frustrating and infuriating for me when she would make assumptions about my motivations or put words in my mouth. Now I feel like she's really getting to know and accept me in a deeper way."

Like Will, your man wants you to see and hear him as an individual. He wants you to respect the fact that he feels the way he feels, even if it's not what *you* think he should be feeling. Men's number-one complaint in relationship is that they don't feel known, understood, and heard by women. We tend to analyze things more than they do, so it's easy for us to dive into their heads and tell them what they're thinking, what they're feeling, and what their motivations are. Imagine how infuriating it might be if your man did this to you. You'd be upset, wouldn't you? Yet you do this to him a lot, maybe without even realizing you're doing it.

Your man longs to be known, understood, and accepted by you. When he doesn't feel recognized or acknowledged, he stops communicating. You then start to wonder, What's wrong that he's not talking? What's wrong is he isn't feeling heard. When you are willing to listen to him and try on his viewpoint, he will be known. When he is known, he will have his heart more open to you. When his heart is more open, he will want to give you what you want. And you will both be happier.

❧ How to Understand Him

Next time your man does something that upsets or confuses you, try the following:

1. Take a deep breath.

2. Relax.

3. Remember that you love him.

4. Assume he is telling the truth.

5. Ask yourself softly and with wonder, "Why does he do that?" The words have a different meaning when they're coming from a loving, curious place.

6. Ask him gently, "Could you help me understand why you do that?"

The benefits of understanding your man far outweigh the effort it takes to let go of "I'm right, you're wrong." He will respond much better to an honest attempt to understand him than to a direct or indirect accusation. He wants you to understand his point of view. It doesn't mean you have to agree with him, just that you agree his perspective is valid. He didn't spend the day figuring out how to bother you. He wants you to be happy. He just does things differently than you do because he is a different person than you are.

Putting yourself in your man's shoes is a practice you can build. It may not be easy at first—new things can be uncomfortable for a while, just as a new pair of shoes needs to be broken in. The more you do it, the more comfortable it will get. The more positive response you get from him, the more encouraged you will be to continue your heartfelt attempt to understand him. It is heart-opening to let yourself really know someone. Your heart will open to your man more and more as you learn about what makes him tick—and he will respond accordingly. When you take the charge out of the question, "Why do you do that?" and ask it from your heart, it's good for you, for him, and for your relationship.

☙ ☙ ☙

List things that upset you about your man.

For each item, ask yourself tenderly, "Why is he like that?"
Contemplate the answer with an open heart.

What is threatening about his inhabiting a different
world than you do?

What would change if you started consciously standing
in your man's shoes?

What are the things you accept, understand, and know
about your man?

What are the things you do not accept, understand,
and know about him?

☙ ☙ ☙

WHO, ME WRONG?

Bridget sighed as she bent over the checkbook. She hated writing checks for the monthly bills, watching hard-earned money flying out the window.

"Why do I always have to be the one to take care of the checkbook, anyway?" Bridget wondered aloud as she stuffed the check into the envelope. "How did I get stuck with this job?"

She licked the envelope and stared absently out the window. Her eyes widened at what she saw. Her husband Jared was lounging on a deck chair in the late-morning sun, reading a magazine.

Outraged, Bridget slapped the envelope in the "outgoing" pile, threw the offending phone bill in the trash, and fumed to herself, I can't believe Jared is relaxing in the sun while I'm sitting here sweating over the bills and wondering how we'll make ends meet this month. He's supposed to be putting together that prefab storage shed out back so I can get the junk out of the front hallway. It's so typical of him to get distracted in the middle of what he's doing. He'll never finish that shed today if he hasn't started yet, and I'll be stuck with piles of junk everywhere for a whole 'nother week!

Bridget stomped out to the patio and let the screen door smack closed behind her. Jared craned his head around to look at her from his lounge chair.

"Oh, hi hon," he said.

"Hi," Bridget said from the doorway, arms folded.

"Something the matter?" Jared asked.

"Well, yeah," Bridget said, rolling her eyes.

"What is it?" Jared asked. "Bills got you down?"

"Mmm," Bridget said.

"Honey, come over here," said Jared. "I'm sorry it stresses you out to pay the bills."

Bridget didn't move. "*You* certainly don't seem stressed," she said pointedly.

Jared looked at her carefully. "No, why should I be?"

"No reason," Bridget said, shifting her weight and tapping her toe.

"Bridget, I can tell you're upset. Won't you let me in on what's wrong?" Jared asked.

Bridget sighed. "I can't believe it's not obvious to you, Jared. I mean, I'm inside sweating over the bills and you're out here lying in the lounge chair."

"So you're saying I should be in there sweating with you?" Jared asked.

"No, I'm saying you should be doing what you promised me you'd do."

Jared just looked at her.

"Putting together the storage shed. Remember? Or has it slipped your mind already?"

"The storage shed," Jared repeated slowly. "So you're upset because you think I'm not working on the shed like I told you I would?"

"I don't *think* you're not working on it, I can *see* you're not working on it."

Jared nodded. "Ah. So you think I've been just lounging around?"

"Are you denying that you've been lying here reading a magazine? I have eyes, you know." Bridget was nearly breathless with exasperation. She couldn't believe Jared was pretending not to know why she was upset when the truth was so blatantly obvious. To top it all off, he looked amused. Surely she wasn't wrong in thinking she saw the beginnings of a smile playing about the corners of his mouth. How could he be laughing about this? He was so immature and irresponsible. She couldn't believe she had ever married such a…a…a *boy!*

"If it weren't for me, this household would have crumbled," she burst out. "Who do you think scrimps and saves so we can have enough money to pay all the bills? Who finds ways to make the place look nice for the least amount of expense? Who keeps the house clean, fixes the meals, even does the plumbing when you're too preoccupied or out with your buddies to do it? Who…"

Bridget suddenly ran out of steam. Jared had picked up the magazine he'd been reading and was holding it up for her to see. It wasn't a magazine at all. It was a thin white flyer, and the black letters emblazoned on the front proclaimed, "How to Assemble Your Storage Shed."

"This is what I was reading," said Jared dryly. "I figured it might be a good idea to know how to put the thing together before starting to bang nails in."

For once, Bridget was speechless. She felt a wave of embarrassment creep up from her toes to her forehead, staining her face red. Suddenly weak, she walked to the chaise and sat down.

"Oh, Jared." She sighed. She didn't know whether to laugh or cry. How could she have been so angry and accusatory when her husband had been out here diligently studying the plans for the shed he was building for her? She'd been so sure she was in the right, so caught up in her wrath, that she hadn't stopped to think maybe she had judged what she was seeing too hastily.

"I'm sorry," Bridget mumbled. "I, um, I guess I was...wrong."

"What?" Jared said. "I didn't quite hear you. Could you repeat that?" He was standing with his arms folded, clutching the manual, a tiny smile playing in the dimples at the corners of his mouth.

He's enjoying this, Bridget thought. She cleared her throat and said clearly, "Honey, I'm sorry. I was wrong."

Bridget felt her heart pounding against her ribs. She hated being wrong more than anything else, and even worse than being wrong was having to admit to someone *else* that she was wrong. She'd rather be righteously angry than wrong, yet she knew she had to let go of her desire to be right in order to resolve this situation. She took a deep breath and felt her heart lighten a bit as she looked up at Jared to see his reaction.

"I'm sorry, I seem to have something in my ear," said Jared. "I thought I heard you say you were sorry, and that you were wrong. Could you say that one more time?"

"Jared," Bridget said, shaking her head and trying not to laugh. "You really know how to make me suffer, don't you? Seriously, though, it's hard for me to admit I'm wrong. You know that. But it actually feels good! I'm relieved."

"Me, too," said Jared.

A Secret to Being Cherished

It's hard to admit we're wrong about something, isn't it? Like Bridget, most of us hate being wrong. It's sometimes easier to work ourselves up into a righteous rage than to have to face the fact that we may be mistaken. We tend to see being wrong as reflecting badly on us. Yet since we are human, it is inevitable that we'll have things we are wrong about. And sometimes it's actually a good thing to be wrong.

If you're going to step into your man's shoes and get to know him better, it may mean you've been wrong about some things. You may have attributed motivations to his actions that are off the mark. In this case, as in Bridget's, it's a good thing to be wrong. When Bridget was sure she was right, she felt justified in being angry with Jared. Being convinced of her righteousness felt good in the moment. Yet in the long run, sticking to her rigid stance could take a serious toll on her relationship. Being able to admit she was wrong turned the scenario around from a potential knock-down, drag-out argument to a moment of fun and intimacy—and a revelation about how she could avoid such upsets in the future.

When things aren't going well, we want someone to blame. Bridget wanted to blame Jared for the stress she was feeling about paying the bills. It made her feel better in the moment—yet if she'd stayed with blaming him, she may have done damage to her relationship. Being willing to be wrong turned the moment around into an opportunity to become more intimate with Jared instead of pushing him away and treating him like the enemy.

It is good to be willing to be wrong. Being willing doesn't mean you necessarily *are* wrong. It just means being open to the possibility of being wrong. And if it's difficult to be willing to be wrong, try being *willing to be willing* to be wrong.

Now is a good time to ask yourself, "Would I rather be right or have a good relationship?"

What are you struggling about with your man?

What is his point of view?

What is yours?

What is hard about being wrong?

Is there something you can be wrong about?

CHAPTER ELEVEN

THIRTEEN FACTS ABOUT MEN

WHO IS THIS LARGE, HAIRY, DEEP-VOICED PERSON in your life? How well do you really know him? Do you want your man to be more like you? Do you get frustrated because he's not? He may seem like a mystery sometimes. Why does he do things differently than you do? It may seem as if he's doing it on purpose to make your life difficult. Yet in all likelihood, your man is *not* trying to drive you crazy. He's just being himself—and he is different from you. Your man would love for you to know him, accept him, and listen to him. He craves your curiosity and wants to be understood. It's worth taking some time to get to know him. He'll act more lovingly when he feels heard, acknowledged, and accepted—and your relationship will improve by leaps and bounds.

As you read this chapter, keep in mind that we are talking in generalities. Yet understanding a few general things can go a long way toward having a healthy relationship. In order to get the most out of the information, then, take it for granted that each quality is followed by the phrase "except for sometimes." That way, you don't have to use your energy thinking, Well, *sometimes* he remembers his cousin's birthday without me telling him. Instead you take in the information as it is meant—as a useful guideline to help your relationship be easier.

1. HE KNOWS HOW POWERFUL YOU ARE.

Your man is well aware of the power you have in his life, even if you don't always realize it yourself. You affect him strongly, and this can frighten him. He is responding to you all the time. Naturally, he wants something loving to respond to. When he doesn't get it, he has no idea what to do except to react in kind. If you're giving him anger to respond to, he may respond in anger.

Your man wants to be your hero. Your appreciation and approval are of supreme importance to him. When you let him be your hero, he feels invincible. How often do you let him feel like a hero? Do you criticize his efforts? When he can't please you, he is crushed. He may not show that he's crushed—in fact, he will probably cover it up really well because he doesn't want you to know how vulnerable he is to you. When he's crushed over and over, he gives up. He may have given up long ago.

This is not something your man is likely to articulate to you, so knowing within yourself how powerful you are is crucial. When you are aware of your power you can afford to be compassionate, and he will respond well to your open heart.

2. HE KNOWS HE IS VULNERABLE TO YOU AND HE CAN'T STAND IT.

Your man is very attached to you, even if he covers it up well.

Believe it! In fact, he may be more attached to you than you are to him—and this scares him. He wants you in his life and he wants to make you happy...and he's terrified that he *can't* make you happy. He doesn't always do the greatest job, does he? He knows this—and it makes him feel vulnerable.

Being vulnerable is very humiliating for your man. He knows he's supposed to be Rambo, and sometimes you make him feel like a lovelorn teenager. Instead of rushing out to save you from enemies, he's trying really hard to please you and failing. What's a man to do? Act macho, of course. The more vulnerable he feels, the more macho he acts. When he says, "I don't care," "It doesn't bother me," "I'm fine," "I'm not jealous," "I don't want to talk about it," or "Nothing's wrong"...don't believe it. He *does* care, terribly. He just can't always afford to show it.

3. SHOWING VULNERABILITY GOES AGAINST WHAT MOST MEN WERE BROUGHT UP TO BELIEVE ABOUT THEMSELVES.

When they were little boys, men learned they should aspire to be superheroes. They were supposed to be unfailingly strong and in control, know the right thing to do and say, and never be emotionally affected by anyone—certainly not a *woman.*

Because little boys don't tend to talk about their fears with each other, they don't realize that they have the same insecurities as other little boys. Your man might have thought he was the only one who couldn't be a superhero, and that may have left him feeling inadequate. He had to hide his feelings underneath a show of macho bravado—and he is still doing that to some extent. How can he admit to you that he feels inadequate when he can't even admit it to himself much of the time?

It is very likely that your man would like to open up to you more, and that the reason he doesn't is that it goes against his belief about how men are supposed to be. Just as you were conditioned to think a prince would come and make your life complete, he was taught that he'd be the one to save you, protect you, and provide for you. His role is to be the defender and provider. That leaves no room for emotional neediness.

Say, for example, that you've asked him to put together a set of shelves you bought at Ikea. He gets frustrated partway through when he can't figure out what to do next. He might say something like, "These directions are stupid. These are ugly shelves anyway. Why don't you just buy some ready-made ones?" You might take it personally and get offended, but it's likely that he's angry at himself for not knowing how to do it right. He hates appearing vulnerable in front of you, so he has to go on the offensive.

The times when your man acts like he doesn't care are probably the times he's feeling the most vulnerable, inadequate, and unheroic. Knowing his dilemma can help you feel compassion for him when he's being distant or difficult. Chances are, that's when he needs your support and love the most. Giving it to him then will encourage him to ask for it more in the future, rather than acting macho or shutting down. And when he's open to you, it will benefit your relationship.

4. HE IS MORE SENSITIVE THAN YOU ARE.

You know how humiliated you feel when you get criticized, especially in public? Multiply that by a hundred and that's how humiliated your man feels. It's true. He may not allow you to see his sensitivity because it doesn't fit in with his belief that he needs to be strong and invulnerable. But believe it—he is acutely sensitive to your treatment of him.

Think of a dog slinking off with its tail between its legs after being chastised. That's how your man feels when you criticize him. He cannot stand your criticism because his ego is very tender. It's a lot more tender than yours because he's supposed to prove at all times how manly he is. When you criticize him, it means he's failed to be your hero, and this damages his sense of his own manhood.

It's bad enough to put down your man in private, but criticize him in public and you can be sure you will experience the repercussions later. It can cause a lot of damage to your relationship to make fun of him or criticize him in front of family or friends. He may laugh along with you, but he will hold it against you for a long time. He may not tell you he's hurt, but he is—and you will pay.

5. When he says something twice, it's important.

Picture you and your man having breakfast one morning. You're reading the paper when out of the blue he says, "I think I would rather have a barbecue than a formal sit-down dinner for our anniversary party next month."

Absorbed in an article, you say, "Mmm, we'll talk about it, honey."

A week later, he brings it up again. "Have you thought about my idea of having a barbecue for the party?"

You nod. "Yes. Hmm. I'm not sure. Listen, I have to get to my appointment. I'm late." And you rush out the door.

You're used to planning all the parties, and you think about the barbecue idea. You talk it over with your mom, and you both agree it should be more formal. You go ahead with plans. The night before the party, your man picks a fight with you over the fact that you left the cap off the toothpaste again. You can't figure out why on earth he's so upset about such a little thing. After a long argument, it finally comes out that he's angry you didn't take his idea about having a barbecue seriously.

You shake your head, mystified. "But I didn't know it was so important to you. I always plan the parties."

"Well, this time I wanted to have some input. What do you mean, you didn't know? I told you twice!"

When you want something or something is bothering you, you tend to dwell on it, right? And since as a woman, you tend to be more vocal than your man about your feelings, you let him know. And let him know. And let him know again. Women have a capacity for dogged persistence when it comes to stating our needs and getting what we want. Chances are, you repeat your needs to him until he gets it. But men aren't necessarily like us when it comes to asking for what they want. If something is really important to your man, he will say it twice. Saying it more than once is big to him. He's made his point, and he expects you've heard him. Yet you may not realize how important it is because he doesn't dwell on it like you do.

When your man says something more than once, it's a good idea to sit up and take notice. He may not say it again because it's humiliating for him to keep asking. And he may hold it against you if you don't consider him. When the subject comes up in six months, he might be adamant, upset, hurt, or angry. You'll say, "If it's that important, why didn't you tell me?" and he'll say, "I *did* tell you." Oops!

6. WHEN UPSET, HE ACTS STRANGELY.

Have you noticed? Your man probably won't sit you down and say, "What you did upset me because..." He's not programmed that way. He wasn't trained to discuss his feelings the way you were, and he may not even be able to articulate them. Instead, he turns into a "bad boy." He will likely do one of four "bad boy" things:

> He will go away emotionally. He's still standing there, but he's gone.

> He will go away physically—for an hour, a day, or a week.

He will start an argument later about something seemingly unrelated.

He will break a promise.

Don't expect your man to confess he's upset. If you ask him what's wrong, he'll probably say, "Nothing." It's not that he's trying to be obtuse. He may not even be aware of what he's doing. He may have no idea that the reason he's picking a fight over dinner tonight is because of a nasty comment you made yesterday. He just knows he's mad about something, and now is the time he's letting it out.

It's up to you to get the signal, make the connection, and find your part. No, it's not fair that once again it's up to you. It's just the way it is. If you want to get to the bottom of his "bad boy" behavior, you'll have to be willing to understand it—because he may not.

Knowing how your man acts when you've upset him will help you deal with it more effectively. Getting upset back at him for his "bad boy" behavior will only make it worse. If you want him to be sweet to you again, understanding him is key. You will be able to say, "Ah, he didn't call me when he said he would. There's my man breaking a promise—he must be upset." Then you can initiate a conversation by saying, "I know I must have done something to upset you." This simple action makes him feel cared about. Your man might respond by saying, "No, what are you talking about? You didn't upset me." In a short time, he'll be back.

7. HE IS COMING FROM A DIFFERENT EXPERIENCE OF LIFE THAN YOU ARE.

Remember when we lived in caves? His brain is formed for spontaneous action, concentrating on the matter at hand, strategizing, and competing. He tends to be more in the moment than you are, and he doesn't dwell on things as much as you do. You think a lot more, analyze situations, and plan for the future. Expecting him to do this the way you do will likely lead to disappointment. When you have a decision to make you can talk about the options for hours with your girlfriends or your sister, right? Say you're looking for a new dining room set. You and your best friend can spend all day going to every furniture store in town, sitting at each table, discussing the merits of different hardwoods, and projecting how much wear and tear the dog or the kids will inflict. Then you can spend another few days checking out all the options in catalogs and online. You might never get tired of discussing it.

You've probably noticed, however, that your man has a much lower tolerance for all this talking, analyzing, projecting into the future, and going back and forth between options than you, your sister, and your girlfriends do. Naturally, you might get offended when he doesn't want to look at all the diningroom sets online or go with you to stores all day Saturday. "You don't care," you tell him. You start thinking maybe he just doesn't want to spend the time with you. Maybe he just doesn't love you enough.

The fact is, though, he is just not built for long decision-making processes. He's much more suited to making quick decisions in the moment. He's very good at it, in fact. It's not that he doesn't care—he just can't weather the process.

Here's what you can do to avoid getting into arguments when you want him to participate in a decision: Look at all the dining room sets yourself or with a friend. Pick out the two you like best. Then ask your man to look at them with you and help you make a decision. He will probably be happy to give you his input because he likes to feel his opinion is valued. And you'll be happy because whichever dining room set he picks, you end up with one of your two favorites. He likes to be included. Voila!

Everyone is satisfied.

Taking into consideration your man's very different experience and orientation will keep you from going down dangerous roads like, "If he loved me enough, he would..." It is more than likely that when you are vexed with his unwillingness to participate, it's simply that it goes against his nature. Step into his shoes for a moment and remember that he is different than you are. When you do this, you can shift the situation so you both end up happy. Isn't it amazing how much power you have?

8. When you have something important to say, keep it brief.

When men are communicating with each other, they tend to be concise and to the point.

"Frank, you want to help me haul some stuff to the dump Saturday?"

"Can't. Got to take one of the kids to soccer practice."

"How about next week sometime, then?"

"Yeah, sure. Thursday evening good for you? Dump's open until seven."

"That works. We could go grab a bite afterward, I'll buy."

"Now you're talking. See ya around six, then?"

"Great. See you then."

Men are very good at getting said what needs to be said with a minimum of words. If two women were having the above conversation, it would probably be a lot longer.

"Sherrie, would you help me take some things to the recycling center Saturday? I have a pile of old stuff in the garage I need to get rid of so I have room for my new car."

"Oh, you're getting a new car? What kind?"

"It's a Honda Accord. It's not really new, it's last year's model, but it's in almost perfect condition. I'm so excited, I've been driving around that ancient Subaru for upwards of eight years now."

"That's great! My sister has an Accord, and she loves it. She's had it for several years and has never had any kind of problem. Besides, they're so attractive. What color is yours?"

"It's called 'heather,' it's kind of a metallic tan, and it has a tan interior."

"Ooh, sounds pretty. Is it an automatic?"

"Yes, thank goodness. Driving in traffic with a standard can be such a drag."

"I know what you mean. Sitting there shifting in and out of first gear. So when are you getting the car?"

"Well, that's the thing. I'm picking it up at the end of next week, so I really need to get this pile of junk out of my garage..."

"Oh yes. Well, I was thinking, why don't you have a garage sale? I know you have some neat things you've been talking about getting rid of. I could help you. I'm really good at going through stuff and organizing it. Besides, I have lots of old baby clothes I wouldn't mind selling."

"Yeah, I thought about that. But I just don't want to go to the trouble of having a sale. I'm so busy right now. And really, Sher, this is just junk. I don't think I could even give it away. You know me, if it's in decent enough shape I'll donate it. But this is bona fide J-U-N-K. Believe me, I just want it out of here."

"Okay, I'm looking at my calendar...Oh, I can't help you this Saturday, I have to take Lizzie to soccer practice. She's got a tournament coming up, you know. Did I tell you her coach thinks she's a very promising player? Anyhow, I promised my sister I'd go over and help her get ready for her party in the afternoon, so I'm totally booked. Oh, I'm sorry. You've helped me out so many times, I feel bad…Listen, how about next Thursday? I know the recycling center is open until seven. We could do it then, and maybe we could catch a bite to eat afterward."

"Good idea, it's been ages since we've hung out to chat. We could go to the Wildflower Café, they have live music Thursday nights. And happy-hour specials. Oh, I guess happy hour will be over by then. Still, they always have good dinner specials. Last time I was there, I had a pasta primavera that was out of this world. And the desserts! I'm a real stickler for a good carrot cake, and I think theirs is the best I've ever had."

"Sounds terrific. I haven't been out in ages. Honestly, I guess I'm getting old. I think the last time I went out with the girls was before Luke was born, can you believe it?"

"Goodness, we need to get you out on the town. But do you have someone to watch the kids?"

"Frank will be home. He'll probably be glad to be rid of me for a night. He'll order a pizza and be happy as can be in front of the TV without me there nagging him. Oh, do you know what he told me the other day? You won't believe it, we laughed and laughed…"

You get the picture.

Since your man is accustomed to relatively brief, succinct communication, it baffles him when you take hours to get your point across. In fact, he probably stops listening after a while because it's overwhelming for him. You are probably all too familiar with that glazed look he gets when you're trying to talk about a serious subject for too long. It's to your benefit to keep important communication as straightforward as possible. He'll be relieved, and will be far more likely to hear you.

9. YOUR MAN FORGETS.

It's probably not unusual for you to find yourself asking, "How could he have *forgotten* that I needed him to pick me up from work today/that I asked him to pick up the dry cleaning/that it's his mother's birthday/that Wednesday is teacher's conferences at school/that I hate mushrooms on my pizza?" You just can't understand why he doesn't remember things, and it drives you crazy. Right?

Your man doesn't forget things *all* the time, but he probably forgets quite a bit—especially the things you really wish he'd remember. In reality, he probably remembers more things than you realize. It's just that you tend to *notice* when he forgets, and you might not notice when he remembers. Because you're only noticing the times he doesn't remember, you might start to think maybe he's forgetting on purpose.

Believe it or not, your man is probably not forgetting things to torture you. There is a biological reason for it. Once again, remember back to the cave times. He didn't develop pathways from past to future in his brain like you did. Your time in the caves trained you in remembering as a survival technique, whereas he didn't have to remember many things. In fact remembering how he did it before may have been detrimental to hunting or fighting. He had to approach each situation with a fresh perspective because he never knew where the animal would charge or how many enemies he'd be facing. Strength and the ability to act spontaneously were the important things.

Men's brains still function differently than ours. If you've noticed, in most couples the woman is the keeper of the social calendar and the grocery list. That's not because men are trying to make our lives miserable by giving us all the scheduling decisions. It's because we are better at it. If you leave the grocery list or the social calendar up to him, it is more than likely you'll end up with no food in the fridge and no plans for Saturday night. That's because it doesn't bother him to have to run out for food, and he doesn't know what he might feel like doing when the weekend comes. He knows this, and he appreciates it when you're willing to be the one to remember.

If you are always waiting for your man to forget and then pouncing on him when he does, it is unpleasant for both of you. Instead of getting frustrated at him for not remembering, why not enjoy the fact that you can do it so efficiently? When he does forget, you can simply say, "Ah, there's my man forgetting." Then you can remember to remind him next time. He is grateful that you remind him about dinner at his brother's or your daughter's tennis tournament, and when he feels grateful he will want to make you happy. Once again, your acceptance of his nature allows him the freedom to be himself, and when he is being accepted, he can open his heart to you instead of being on the defensive.

10. HE HAS A DIFFERENT SENSE OF TIME THAN YOU DO.

"Tammy, I'm worried. You know Rick's on a business trip, and he said he'd call when he arrived today. He hasn't called. What if something's happened?"

"It's only three o'clock in the afternoon, Rhonda. Maybe he couldn't call you until later."

"But he *said* he'd call when he got in. He was supposed to arrive at his hotel around noon. Oh no, his plane crashed, I know it. I saw on the news that they were having terrible storms in Minneapolis."

"I'm sure he's fine, Rhonda. He'll call soon, I'm sure."

"Oh, there's my call waiting! I'll bet that's him. I can't believe he waited this long to call. Grrr! Gotta go."

Does Rhonda's scenario sound familiar? There have probably

been times when you and your man got into disagreements about timing. He said he'd call, or he'd do something by a certain time, and he didn't do it. It's infuriating, isn't it? It seems as if he's purposely trying to drive you crazy. The good news is, he's *not*.

"Tomorrow," "later," "this afternoon," and even "ten-thirty" may mean something different to your man than they do to you. When something happened three weeks ago, it might seem to him like it happened last week. Why? Because back in the caves, he didn't have to develop the complex sense of past and future that you did. Spontaneity was his ally, and it still is. To someone who lives in the moment as much as he does, time has a different meaning.

Since you're the one with the sense of urgency, you're the one who has to take the initiative. He doesn't have the same sense of urgency that you do. If you want something done soon, ask him ahead of time. Then praise him lavishly when he does it. This is a far more efficient method than nagging, which only gets him defensive. Since he craves your approval, if you praise him he'll want to finish a project on time when you ask him next. And he doesn't mind being reminded as long as you're not criticizing while you're doing it.

11. HE IS SIMPLER THAN YOU ARE.

You are more complicated than your man. Women in general are very complex, and we have a lot of thoughts in a day. You might have noticed that you're more verbal than your man. What does it mean that you have so many more words cross your mind in a day? It does *not* mean you are superior to him, tempting as that belief might be. More is not necessarily better. How many thoughts do we have in a day that are really meaningful or insightful? Most of our thoughts aren't all that important. They can even be damaging, as in the following scenario.

Imagine you have an argument with your man in the morning before you both leave for work. As you go about your day, your mind is continually going over the argument. "What did he mean when he said that? Could he be falling out of love with me? He did say something strange last week. How could he say these things to me? I can't believe it. He has no idea how good he has it with me." Et cetera.

While you are busy creating World War Three in your head, chances are your man is simply getting on with his workday. He is really good at focusing on the task at hand and putting other matters out of his mind. When you get home at night, you might be simmering with resentment, and he is as fresh as a daisy because he hasn't been obsessing all day. He might even have forgotten all about the argument. In all likelihood, he has not spent his day thinking about everything that's wrong with you or obsessing about what you meant by the word "blue." It might be infuriating to you that he's not focused on your relationship troubles all the time...but think about it. Isn't it better that he's not? You know what a stew you can get in about the littlest thing. Chances are, he doesn't get into the same stew. Think what a mess you'd be in if you were *both* thinking about your latest argument all day.

It is relatively easy to make your man feel like a king. He doesn't require the same level of emotional upkeep that you do. He doesn't think about what you think about all day. It's relatively effortless for him to be in the moment and enjoy the simple things in life. He wants your pleasant company, and he wants to feel cared for. It's worth considering, isn't it? When he feels like a king, he'll want to spread his largesse around. And there you'll be!

12. YOU HAVE THINGS TO LEARN FROM YOUR MAN.

It's true! His simplicity is a gift you can benefit from. He's good at a lot of things that can make life lighter and more fun. When you're not using up your energy being annoyed with him for not being like you, it can be really stimulating to discover new ways of doing things. And he'll be flattered you want to do them with him.

Things You Can Learn From Your Man

SPONTANEITY. Impromptu picnic at the beach? He'll have you in the car, sunroof open, and a cooler of treats in the backseat in no time. Need to make a quick decision in a family emergency? He's likely to do it, and do it well. You probably feel more comfortable having everything planned out ahead of time, but life doesn't always work that way. His ability to be spontaneous and go with the flow is a great asset, and one you can benefit from emulating at times.

ENJOYING SIMPLE PLEASURES. Because he's better at being in the present than you are, he can really soak up a moment. A nap in the sun, a good song on the radio, a kiss, an ice cream cone…your man is the one to help you appreciate the small things in life.

BEING PLEASABLE. He can be like a little kid when he gets a gift, can't he? He'll play with that remote control car for hours, or tootle around happily on his tractor mower all afternoon. When you bring him a glass of iced tea, he's delighted. When you give him a kiss after he takes a sip, he's thrilled. It doesn't take a lot to make him happy. Your good mood is often enough. He sets a great example by his willingness to be pleased. You're a lot harder to please—and that makes it hard for him to want to give to you. Try being easy to please for a while, and see how much more fun you can have.

TAKING THINGS LIGHTLY. When you're upset or in a crisis, your man is the one who will likely try to lighten the mood with humor. It may seem to you that he's not taking the situation seriously enough, yet the opposite is probably true. He's aware of how seriously you're taking it, and he is using humor to try to make you feel better. It would be good for you to follow his lead sometimes. Let some laughter lighten the atmosphere...and suddenly, things don't look so dire anymore.

LETTING THINGS ROLL OFF HIS BACK. He's far better at shrugging it off when something upsetting happens. He doesn't analyze things as much as you do. Because he isn't spending all day thinking about what went wrong, he's happier.

HAVING FUN. Your man may well be a natural at game-playing. Because he's more spontaneous, he can really enjoy having fun in the moment. Why not let him enrich your life with some simple fun and games?

13. HE WANTS YOU TO BE HAPPY.

When your man says, "I just want you to be happy," believe him. Men know instinctively what women have to learn by trial and error: When you're happy, he's happy. When you're content, the relationship is going well. When you aren't happy, he panics. Perhaps it reminds him of seeing his mother be unhappy when he was a child and being unable to help her. Today, when he doesn't know what to do to make you happy he has the same feeling of helplessness. If what he tries doesn't work he gives up quickly. He feels like a failure and he can't stand it, so he just closes up shop.

To put it simply, your man wants you to feel good in his presence for two reasons:

> 1. He knows his life is easier when you are happy.
>
> 2. When you feel good in his presence, he feels like a hero.

Your happiness is a gift you can give him. Isn't that great? All you have to do is allow yourself to be pleased, and your man is thrilled. Then he wants to do more to please you because he loves it when you're happy. It makes your man feel like a million bucks to see you enjoying yourself. He feels personally responsible for your happiness. He wants to be included in the great life you've created for yourself.

Being pleasable is not necessarily an inherited skill. You might have to work at it a little. That means letting him do what he wants to do to make you happy, and accepting his efforts graciously. See that he is giving to you with love, no matter what it is he's giving. Then when he gives it to you, thank him. Show him how happy he's made you. He will be proud and pleased, and will want to make you happy again. It becomes a delightful circle of give and take that benefits you, him, and the relationship. When you allow him to make you happy, he will do anything for you.

❦ ❦ ❦

Review each of the thirteen points.

How can you use each point to make your relationship be the one you want?

Which three will you begin using first? List them.

Acknowledge to yourself where you made a shift. Remember that shifts can be subtle.

Notice his response.

❦ ❦ ❦

Chapter Twelve

How to Talk with Your Man

"We need to talk." Those may be the four words men dread most. Why? Because they know they must have done something wrong. They get on the defensive because they know we are more verbal and can often argue circles around them. They know that when we say, "We need to talk," we have a lot to communicate, and it can be overwhelming for them. When you want to have a productive discussion with your man, then, you need a strategy that allows you to get your point across in a way it works for you—*and* have him be able to tolerate listening to it.

Men like a conversation to be brief. In this case, less is more. That's where the "fifteen-minute rule" comes into play. It's a simple concept that allows you and your man to communicate most effectively. It's simple: If you want to have a productive talk with your man, *keep intense or important conversations to a fifteen-minute limit.*

Instead of "We need to talk," say to him, "I'd like to have a conversation with you for fifteen minutes." If he knows you won't be talking for hours, he will be more likely to really listen. If what you have to say takes longer than fifteen minutes, don't go on. Instead, tell him you have more to say and schedule another fifteen-minute session for another day. Then get up and leave. He will be relieved that you stuck to your word, and more willing to sit down and have a fifteen-minute talk the next time.

You may have a lot to say after reading this book. What you have to say will probably be different from what you've been accustomed to saying, and it may be a little surprising to your man at first. He is going to need some time to get used to your new perspective. It may be frustrating at first to have to stop in the middle of what you're saying, yet in the long run you will be fixing things between you.

✒ The Fifteen-Minute Rule

In order to have a productive conversation with your man about something important, use the following recipe for success:

Decide which part of what you want to say is most important to say right now, and save the rest for another time.

Go over in your mind what you want to say. Breathe. Check to make sure that to the best of your ability you have your heart open, you are owning your part, you are willing to listen to his side, and you are not blaming anyone.

Approach your man lovingly. Ask him when would be a good time for a fifteen-minute conversation.

Respect his time schedule. If he doesn't want to talk right now and you force it, you will be a lot less likely to end up with the result you want from the conversation. Take care of yourself and make sure you schedule a time that works for you, too.

When it's time, sit down with him in a quiet place where you won't be disturbed. Let him know that the conversation will be only fifteen minutes. This will allow him to relax because he'll know he won't be on the spot for hours.

Have your heart open to him. Talk calmly and lovingly, and listen fully.

After fifteen minutes, be the one to end the conversation. If the conversation is not finished, make an appointment for another fifteen-minute slot later or on another day.

It may be hard at first to have to stop the conversation or keep it within a time limit. Yet you'll be amazed at how efficiently you can solve your problems with your man when you adhere to the fifteen-minute rule. He will respond much better to this short, structured, loving conversation than to a long, drawn-out, emotionally draining conversation. And it takes a lot less out of you, too. You will be improving your relationship—fifteen minutes at a time.

HE SAYS "PO-TAY-TO," YOU SAY "PO-TAH-TO"

You use language differently than your man does. Have you noticed? A word or phrase might mean one thing to you and another thing to him. Words are rarely just words, especially when you're talking about a serious subject. They become charged with meaning through your experience of life. When you're wondering what could possibly have provoked his reaction to a simple statement or request you made, it's probably because he interpreted it differently. You do the same thing—it's unavoidable.

> For example:
> She says, "Let's talk."
>> He hears, "I'm in trouble."
>
> He says, "Let's talk."
>> She hears, "He wants something from me."
>
> She says, "Why did you do that?"
>> He hears, "She's blaming me."
>
> He says, "Why did you do that?"
>> She hears, "He thinks there's something wrong with me."

She says, "Let's get married."
> He hears, "Marriage is the death of a good relationship."

He says, "Let's get married."
> She hears, "We'll end up just like my parents."

She says, "I want to have kids."
> He hears, "I'll have to make a lifetime commitment."

He says, "I want to have kids."
> She hears, "He wants to keep me tied to the house."

She says, "Why don't we buy a new car?"
> He hears, "She doesn't like my trusty Ford."

He says, "Why don't we buy a new car?"
> She hears, "We'll be throwing money away."

When your words collide, it can feel like the end of the world. It is useful to remember that you are two separate beings, with your own interpretations of what each other does and says. Not only that, your man communicates differently than you do. It's not just that he has fewer words cross his mind in a day or that he has a shorter tolerance for intense conversations. Sometimes he says things in a sort of "man-code" that you may be hard-pressed to understand. Following is a key to "manspeak" that will help you communicate more effectively with him.

"I don't know how to do this" means "Tell me in detail, nicely." And you may have to tell him more than once—gently and with care.

"I don't care, you decide" can mean two things. If he says it at the beginning of a conversation, he means, "I don't care, you decide." The decision's not important to him, and he would rather have you decide so that you will be happy with your decision. If he says it at the end of a long, exhausting conversation and you have exasperated him by your persistence, it probably means, "I am more interested in ending this conversation than in discussing it anymore or getting my way."

"How could you think I would think that?" means, "How can you not know me? I love you and I'm doing the best I can."

"If I do what you ask, will you be happy?" means, "I'm willing to play the game and give you what you want—but then you can't complain."

"I'm willing to try doing what you want" means, "Give me the benefit of the doubt. If I'm not doing it well, remind me gently."

"I don't want to talk about this anymore right now" means he really wants the conversation to stop. It's probably getting too intense for him. His feelings are strong and he's afraid he'll say something he doesn't mean. He may also be afraid you'll say something to hurt him or something he doesn't want to know. If it's a really heated discussion, he may fear that his anger will get out of control and he'll explode. He doesn't want to hurt you. So when he asks for a conversation to stop, grant him his desire. It's better for both of you in the long run. Later, try to make an appointment for a future fifteen-minute conversation.

"This hurts" means "Stop talking. Find another way to say the same thing in a way that I can hear and be empowered by." You can mark this as a place that probably needs healing and remember to stay awake and gentle when approaching this subject again. There is something to learn about your man here. Pay attention, be sweet with one another, and stay awake.

"Do you think it's possible to work this out?" means, "This is a trouble spot. Please be careful here; I need your help. Reassure me that we can work this out."

When You're Talking to Your Man...

Be aware that the language you use in conversation with your man has an impact on the vibration, or energy, you are giving out. He will respond to your vibration, so it is worth your while to choose your words with care. When you do this, you are creating a new habit that's worth having.

Here are some suggestions for language that puts your relationship into a positive context instead of a combative one—whether you're having a conversation with yourself or with him.

Instead of... Say...

"This is difficult."
　　"This is stimulating."

"Why do you always..."
　　"Your puzzle piece fits mine."

"We're fighting."
　　"Here's an opportunity to heal the past."

"It's your fault."
　　"Thank you for giving me another chance to learn about myself."

"I feel bad and I can't stand it."
　　"I'm feeling bad so a good thing can happen."

"This problem is insurmountable."
　　"We are two rough stones rubbing together."

"It would be different with someone else."
　　"It's here to be healed, and if I don't do it now it will come up again in another situation."

Guidelines for Conversations With Your Man

BE AWARE OF YOUR TONE OF VOICE. He listens to your tone of voice first, *then* what you are saying. Your tone of voice is an indicator of your mood, and he is constantly monitoring your moods so he knows how to respond. If your tone is accusatory, critical, judgmental, angry...he is likely to get on the defensive and either stop listening or attack. If you're saying something in a neutral or loving tone of voice, he will be more likely to participate in the conversation. Being as calm as possible will allow you to get your point across and have him hear it.

LISTEN TO HIM. Since you are likely more verbal than he is, it's easy to override what he's saying. Take a deep breath, lean back, and listen. Don't assume you know what he is going to say or jump in and finish his sentences for him. Find out about your man. Let him surprise you.

BELIEVE HIM. Remember that he's standing in different shoes than you are, and he is speaking *his* reality. Honor his reality the way you would like him to honor yours, and you will be setting a loving example.

SAVE YOUR ARGUMENTS FOR THE THINGS

WORTH ARGUING ABOUT. He gets desensitized after a while if you're dissatisfied with him. If something is trivial, be willing to let it go. Ask yourself, "Is it worth arguing about which way the dishes should go in the cupboard?" Distinguishing the arguments worth having gives more power to the times when you really have something important to say.

DON'T USE "ALWAYS" OR "NEVER." Those are fighting words!

LEARN TO SAY THE FOLLOWING PHRASES:

"I made a mistake."

"I'm sorry."

"It's my fault."

"I was worried about you."

"I'm having fun."

"This is better than I ever thought it could be."

"I'm lucky to have such a great life."

These phrases are worth practicing. They may feel awkward at first, so say them to yourself in the mirror, in the shower, in the car. Why? Because these are the phrases that will allow you to have the life-affirming conversations necessary for your relationship to flourish. It is empowering to have loving conversations because they allow you to have the relationship you both deserve.

❦ ❦ ❦

Think back to the last upset you had with your man.

What if you had used the information in this chapter?

Can you see that you might have had a different result?

Practice one fifteen-minute conversation with your man.

Pick several points from this chapter and begin
practicing them.

Try at least one fifteen minute conversation with your
man this week.

❦ ❦ ❦

Chapter Thirteen

WORKING TOGETHER

A RELATIONSHIP THAT'S WORKING WELL CONTAINS a certain amount of disagreement. It's healthy to express yourselves and deal with differences. In fact, if there are never any trouble spots, it may mean the two of you aren't really connecting. It is good for your relationship to be able to trust each other to deal with disagreements. When you have issues to talk over, you can come up with a solution together—and become more intimate in the process.

As you continue to nurture your relationship, expect differences to arise. A problem-free life exists only in fantasy. Yet problems don't have to tear you apart if you are prepared to handle them together. When your heart is open and you are seeing your relationship as a place where both of you can be taken care of, you and your man can find solutions to your issues without having them cause major rifts between you. In fact, working on a problem together and coming up with a solution can be a process of teamwork that ultimately strengthens your relationship.

Since it's healthy to deal with the issues, you will want to do it in a way that strengthens and deepens your relationship. Following are some ways of solving issues and differences that *work*:

ASSUMING HE IS NOT THE ENEMY

Vanessa pulled her pink cashmere sweater out of the dryer, staring at it ruefully. It had shrunk so much it looked like a toddler's sweater.

"I can't believe Raymond put my sweater in the dryer," she muttered to herself. "How could he do this to me?"

Holding up the sweater like an accusatory beacon, Vanessa marched into the living room.

"Raymond, could you explain this?" she asked, standing in front of him with the tiny sweater held up to her chest.

"Umm, not really," he said absently, looking up from the Sunday *Times*. "What is it? One of the kids' sweaters?"

Vanessa snorted. "Well, that's what it looks like, doesn't it? But it's not. In fact, Ray, this is—or *was*—my best cashmere sweater. It cost over a hundred dollars. It's supposed to be hand-washed."

"Oh," Raymond said, recognition dawning. "I guess I must have thrown it in the wash with the rest of the colored load. Gosh, I'm sorry."

"I don't know if sorry is going to cut it," Vanessa said. "I can't replace this sweater with 'sorry.'"

"Well, what do you want me to do?" asked Raymond. "I can't

undo what I did. I was trying to help you out by doing the wash because I knew you were really busy with that project at work. So I shrunk your sweater."

Vanessa slowly lowered the sweater, looking into Raymond's eyes. He really did look sorry, and she could tell he felt badly.

"Oh, well, it's just a sweater," she said, tossing it aside with a halfhearted laugh. "I know you were just trying to help. I guess your five-year-old daughter just got a new sweater."

"Come here, hon," Raymond said, moving aside the *Times* to make room for her next to him on the couch. "Listen, I'll buy you a new sweater, okay?"

Vanessa sank down next to him, giving him a hug. "Thanks, Ray. I'm sorry I accused you. I forget sometimes that we're on the same team."

"Team Us, remember?" Raymond said, using the name they'd coined at the beginning of their marriage to remind themselves they were in it together.

"Team Us," Vanessa agreed.

What allowed Vanessa to switch her energy from being annoyed to being loving? She caught herself in the act of treating Raymond like the enemy, and she reminded herself that he was on her side. Seeing the effect her accusatory tone had on him, she was able to open her heart and forgive him. In doing this, she was able to transform a potentially devastating argument into a brief disagreement that allowed them to become more intimate.

Your man is not in your life to make you miserable. He is not the enemy. He's doing the best he can, and he needs your understanding and forgiveness just as you need his. When you come from a place of assuming he is on your side, you can single-handedly turn arguments into healing opportunities for both of you. He doesn't want to be arguing either. He doesn't enjoy having altercations with you. He will respond well when you are willing to see him as your ally, and your relationship will have much more room to blossom.

AVOIDING "WHO'S RIGHT, WHO'S WRONG" CONVERSATIONS

If Vanessa hadn't caught herself in the act of treating Raymond like the enemy, she could easily have sucked them both into a vortex of blaming each other. Instead of finding resolution, the conversation could have turned into something like the following:

"Why couldn't you have checked with me before just throwing everything into the washing machine?" Vanessa asks, annoyed.

"The whole point was, I was trying to help you out," Raymond says with exasperation.

"Well, it ended up being a disaster instead of a help," Vanessa replies. "Can't you do anything right?"

"As a matter of fact, I do a lot of things right. Why can't you see that I was just trying to help you? Maybe you shouldn't have thrown your precious sweater in with the rest of the laundry. If it's that delicate, you should have put it somewhere else."

"Oh, so now it's my fault that you shrunk my sweater!"

"Well, if you weren't so careless with your things, it wouldn't have been ruined."

Can you see what a powerful effect Vanessa's attitude has on the course of the discussion? When she wasn't listening with an open heart, Raymond felt blamed and got defensive. Now, the argument might well escalate into an altercation that could last all day or all week, with blame being slung around on both sides.

It is always best to avoid "who's to blame" conversations. They almost always lead to upsets. Instead, take a breath and start from, "Here we are. Now what can we do?" Be willing to be wrong, own your part, and have your heart open. You'll thank yourself later.

PUTTING THE PROBLEM OUTSIDE
THE TWO OF YOU

A few days later, Vanessa and Raymond began planning their vacation. They agreed that they wanted to go on a cruise together. However, they couldn't agree on where to go. Raymond wanted to go on an Alaskan cruise and Vanessa wanted to go on a Caribbean cruise.

"But Alaska is cold," Vanessa objected when Raymond told her his desire.

"It's not cold in the summer. We could go in June. It's so beautiful up there, and it's our one chance to see the Alaskan wilderness."

"I don't want to see the Alaskan wilderness," Vanessa countered. "When you said cruise, I was picturing lying in the sun, getting out to snorkel and nose around in the markets of Caribbean ports. Doesn't that sound fun?"

"It does, but what about seeing glaciers? With global warming, they won't always be around, you know. And you can take great day trips off the ship. You can even go on helicopter explorations of the glaciers!"

"The glaciers aren't going anywhere in our lifetime, Raymond. It's so typical of you to exaggerate in order to get your way." Vanessa was starting to lose her patience as she saw her dream of a tropical cruise slipping away.

"What do you mean, it's typical of me to exaggerate? I never exaggerate. I'm stating a scientific fact. I didn't say anything about the glaciers melting during our lifetimes. You always misinterpret what I'm saying. I swear you do it deliberately!"

"I do not. You misled me. You said, 'Honey, let's go on a cruise.' You knew I'd think of going somewhere warm. When on Earth have I ever wanted to go somewhere cold on vacation? How could you be so selfish?"

"Vanessa, calm down. You're overreacting, as usual, and ignoring the facts. Alaska in the summer is not cold! It's beautiful. You can be out in the sun."

"I am not overreacting. You never take my feelings into consideration. Just because you're completely rational at all times doesn't mean the rest of us don't have feelings!" Vanessa is on the verge of tears.

Raymond sighed. "It's obvious we're not going to get anywhere talking about this. It's deteriorated into emotional indulgence, as usual. What's so wrong with being rational? At least I can have an adult conversation without bursting into tears."

"You're cruel!" Vanessa sobs. "I can't believe I'm with someone so unfeeling." And she ran out of the room.

What happened to Vanessa and Raymond's discussion? They started out talking about the issue of where to go on vacation, and they ended up arguing about each other. For Vanessa, Raymond had become the problem. For Raymond, Vanessa had become the problem. Instead of partners discussing an issue, they had become enemies attacking each other.

When a discussion with your man turns into an argument, it's because a problem has come between you. You are no longer partners who are on the same team, wanting each other to be happy. You become opponents trying to defeat one another. The original issue you were discussing has become beside the point, and the problem becomes each other.

What can you do instead? Imagine the problem as a ball sitting between you and your man. Remove the ball from between you and set it a few feet away. Then get on the same side of it, as partners. Literally, get up and sit together, holding hands and facing the problem. When you are side by side, you are on the same team. The problem is no longer each other. It is an entity in itself, and it has a name.

Vanessa and Raymond's problem is called, "How can we enjoy a great vacation together and ensure we both have our needs met?" They could make the problem real by taking some cruise brochures and setting them on the coffee table. Then they could sit beside each other on the sofa. Now they are united as a team, facing the problem together—and they can have a discussion rather than an argument. Instead of getting personal and attacking each other, they can focus on the problem at hand, listen to each other, and find a solution that works for both of them.

"I don't know, Raymond. Alaska is too cold, even in July. I want to be hot on my vacation, I'm so sick of this cold weather."

"But the Caribbean isn't as interesting as Alaska. Alaska has glaciers, and you can take helicopter trips to see them up close. Honestly, Vanessa, how could you want to go somewhere as banal as the Caribbean?"

"I don't think the Caribbean is banal."

"But everyone goes to the Caribbean on a cruise. Can't you be just a little bit original for once?"

Vanessa takes a deep breath, reminding herself to keep her heart open. She says gently, "Raymond, the problem is where to go on vacation. The problem is not me, and it's not you. It's over there, on the coffee table. Remember?"

Raymond nods grudgingly. "Okay, but I still think Caribbean islands are boring."

"So you want to go somewhere with geographical interest?"

"Yes."

"Well, how about Mexico? It's warm, and there's the jungle and all the Mayan ruins."

"Hmm, that's an idea. It's not wilderness like in Alaska, but there is some interesting terrain there. And the ruins are intriguing."

"Yes, and you can hike in the jungle while I lie on the beach."

"It doesn't sound like a bad idea...Hey, how about Belize? I've heard it has some great ruins, and you can take lots of interesting trips inland. They have those howler monkeys that have always interested me."

"Sure, Belize would be great. Either one could be a good solution. As long as there's a beach."

"And hikes. Okay, let's do some more research and talk about it again."

Now Vanessa and Raymond have a common ground to stand on next time they talk about their vacation. They've established an attitude of partnership. The charge has been taken out of their interaction, and some resolution is possible. In fact, they have the possibility for a creative solution—one they may never have come up with when they were busy being angry at each other. It's easier to come up with creative solutions when you're not upset with each other.

Name a problem you and your man are having.

What would happen if you set the problem outside you and approached it as a team?

GIVING HIM THE PROBLEM HE GIVES YOU

Sometimes a problem arises that you just can't seem to resolve. When he can't seem to understand your needs or you have opposing needs, what can you do? *Give him the problem he is giving you.* Giving him back the problem means enlisting his help in finding a solution.

Vanessa can't stand it that Raymond is always late. It's been bothering her for a while, and they've had several arguments about it. Raymond argues that he always tries his best to be on time, but that he's often running late because of his hectic schedule. Vanessa contends that Raymond should be able to budget his time better so he doesn't keep her waiting.

One night when she's been waiting at a restaurant for half an hour with no sign of her husband, Vanessa decides she is tired of the situation. She doesn't want to wait for him every time they make plans, and she also doesn't want to argue about it anymore. When Raymond shows up, she greets him with a kiss and gives him time to settle into his seat.

After they order drinks, Vanessa says, "Honey, I need your help. It's really hard on me when you're late, especially when we make plans for a special date like tonight. I look forward to see- ing you at the end of the day, and it's disappointing when you don't show up for so long. Also I get anxious while I'm waiting, and I worry that something's happened to you. It's not a pleas- ant situation for me. What can we do?"

Vanessa has just given Raymond back the problem he gave her. She doesn't want it anymore, and she has asked for his help in dealing with it. He can now help her come up with a solution instead of having to defend himself against an attack.

When you give your man the problem he gave you, three

things occur:

1. He has the opportunity to step into your shoes for a moment. Your heartfelt description of the situation allows him to see what it is like for you.

2. He feels valued because you are treating him as an intelligent and able person.

3. He can feel like a hero if he can come up with a solution. If he doesn't come up with a solution, at least he has a better understanding of the problem. He may come up with a solution in a few days...or you might.

Giving your man the problem allows him to be involved. He feels great when you listen to him and assume he has valuable input. He wants to be a partner in this relationship, just as you do. When you include him rather than attack him, he has a chance to come up with an answer. Men are competitive by nature and love finding solutions. Why not let him use his natural ability for your benefit? Even if he doesn't have an answer, he will appreciate that you asked. Next time the problem comes up, he will be more understanding. It may need to come up several more times before you reach a solution, but the two of you can approach it as a team rather than as opponents.

Think of a situation with your man where you don't feel your needs are getting met.

What would happen if you gave him back the problem?

Write out what you would say.

Committing to Working It Out

If either Vanessa or Raymond had been halfway out the door, they wouldn't have been able to resolve their problems. "We'll see what happens" can't fix a relationship. It takes two of you with your feet planted firmly inside the relationship in order to work things out. In fact, the only way to see if your relationship is fixable is for you both to have your feet in the door for a period of time with no thought of leaving.

Be willing for things to work. Arrange with your man to commit to three months where neither of you will consider leaving. For those three months, act as if your only option is to work it out within the relationship. If you need to, extend the period to six months or more. You both deserve a safe place to work it out where there's no threat of either of you leaving. While you're in your three- or six-month span, have your attitude be, "How are we going to fix it?" Are you willing to do what it takes to have your relationship work out? (And if you aren't willing, why would he be?)

Checklist for Working on Issues

In order to have a productive discussion of an issue...

1. Be willing to step into your man's shoes.

2. Remember that his point of view makes sense to him.

3 Don't assume that you are right and he's wrong.

4. Listen and be fascinated to learn something new about him.

5. Be as open to hearing about him as you were early on in the relationship.

6. Be committed to working it out with no threat of anyone leaving for a period of time.

7. Work as if you are a team.

8. He won't be able to resist following your lead and responding in kind!

CHAPTER FOURTEEN

PITFALLS, OR WHAT TO WATCH OUT FOR

ALMOST ALL OF US HAVE WOKEN UP at some point to find ourselves wondering: *How did I get here? How can I get out?*" This chapter will provide you with quick help for those times when you find yourself scrabbling for a foothold in your relationship. Often the problem is that you've hit a pitfall—something you do without even realizing it that can cause a lot of mischief.

Following is a list of the top ten most common pitfalls for women. You may not fall into all the pits in the list, but certainly some will seem familiar. As you read, keep yourself open to discovering your own pitfalls. Knowing what they are will benefit your relationship, because it will help you be awake and aware when you start sliding into behavior that may be damaging. Instead of feeling helpless, you'll know you have the power to sidestep the pitfall and to stop the downward slide.

Pitfall #1: Waiting for the prince

From an early age, you were promised a fairy tale—a prince who would sweep you away to live in the land of Happily-Ever-After. Hollywood, romance novels, theater, magazines, love songs, and maybe even your mother all conspired to keep you waiting for a prince—a man of practically superhuman strength, charm, wit, and looks. No matter what era you were raised in, the expectation remained the same: You would meet your prince someday and he'd make your life complete. He would provide you with everything you needed to be happy, and the two of you would ride off into the sunset together.

Expecting a prince instead of a human being is among the most harmful pits women fall into. Holding real, live men up to a fantasy ends many relationships—before *and* after marriage.

No matter how long you've been with your man, you may *still* be waiting for a prince. When things aren't going well, it's almost instinctive to begin comparing your man to a list of princely qualities—no matter how aware you are. Intellectually you may know a man won't be enough to make your life complete. You probably realize that no human being can be perfect. Yet when you were a child you bought into the fairy tale hook, line, and sinker—and that young girl hasn't gone anywhere. She's still inside you somewhere, waiting for her prince to come. And she's disappointed in the man you've ended up with. Of course, when she was watching *Cinderella*, she never got a chance to see how the prince behaved once he was settled into daily life in the castle. The story ended conveniently before the happy couple had to divide up the chores, share a bathroom, or plan where to take a vacation.

We want to blame men for not being princes, but *we* are the ones that confer princely status, or lack thereof. It's all in our heads. To the extent that you are still waiting for the prince to come, you will be dissatisfied and disappointed in your man. Only when you throw away the list of ideal qualities you're holding onto will you be able to start appreciating and accepting him for who he is. And this paves the way for greater ease and happiness in your relationship.

ও ও ও

What are the movie, television, and literature heroes you have from childhood, teen years, and as a young adult, that may be still influencing you today?

What did these heroes promise you?

What was the most important image you took on that you now use to compare your man to?

ও ও ও

Pitfall #2: Living up to a picture

As a child, was there someone you admired, whose life you envied or aspired to? It could have been a fictional life from a television show or a book, a celebrity, a friend's parent, a teacher, or another adult you admired. Perhaps you took bits from several different scenarios and created an ideal future for yourself in your mind. However it looked, you took a mental snapshot of that ideal. You may not even remember doing it, but nearly everyone has a picture of an ideal life they hold up in comparison to the life they're living. And it is very likely that you are still holding on to that snapshot—even if you don't realize it.

Your picture keeps you from knowing what you really want.

Perhaps, for instance, you always admired your best friend's aunt, who never married and traveled frequently to exotic locales. You longed to be like her when you were a child, and now that you're married, there is still a part of you attached to that longing. You find yourself getting angry if you don't get to travel overseas every year—even if you don't really want to anymore. Why? Because not traveling doesn't fit the picture you formed as a child.

That snapshot may obscure what is true for you now. If you're not sure that you're living a life that is authentic for you, ask yourself, "What is right for me today?"

What is right for you now may not be what was right for you two years ago or what will be right for you in a year. Because you're a dynamic human being, your desires shift. You are living in an exciting time where you can choose the life you want. And you have the power to draw into your life what it is you really want—now, today, as the adult you are.

What does all this have to do with your relationship? Comparing your real life to your ideal life may contribute to a feeling of dissatisfaction with your man. You may find yourself blaming your husband for the fact that your life doesn't feel good to you. It's natural to want someone to blame, yet it's important to remember that your man did not sign up for the job of making your life fit your ideal. He was not put on Earth to make you happy. How can he fulfill every one of your needs when he can barely take care of his own? Yes, he wants you to be satisfied—*and* your happiness is up to you.

Getting rid of your "ideal" snapshot will give you the freedom to develop a new, supportive picture of your life. You can reassure the little girl who created the picture that you have many good things in your life that never could have been there if you'd stuck to the snapshot. Your life can be good the way it is. And you can create room for your man in that picture—just as he is. Chances are, you already have a lot of what you want. You just may not have seen it because that snapshot was taking up all the room.

🍂 🍂 🍂

Have you been measuring your life against an ideal?

What are the pictures of that ideal, exactly?

Are these snapshots authentic for you now?

Which should you let go of?

What is working well in your life that you never could have foreseen?

🍂 🍂 🍂

Pitfall #3: Treating him as an object

When you first got involved with your man and were getting to know him, you probably treated him as someone special. You responded to his needs, did what you could to make him comfortable, listened to him carefully, soothed him when he needed tenderness, showed him often that you loved him, and went out of your way to care for him. And he did the same for you.

So what changed?

As a relationship settles into a routine, people often stop treating each other as special and start taking each other for granted. As you get comfortable in the relationship and spend more and more time together, the little "extras" can tend to drop off. Daily life often takes over, and it doesn't seem as important or necessary to make a special effort.

What you might have missed is that *you* may have also stopped treating *him* as someone special. At first your loving attention made him feel great, and he wanted to be around you as much as possible. In all likelihood, though, most of the things you used to do to demonstrate your love have fallen by the wayside. Instead, you've gradually come to expect that he would be there for you when you needed him, do his duties and chores, leave you alone when you needed him to, make a showing at social events, and generally be an asset to your life. He becomes a useful appendage whose main purpose is to help fill your needs.

Think about the last time you were planning a party, a family get-together, or a social outing. Did you take your man's needs into consideration, or did you go ahead and plan it without consulting him? When you are dealing with your kids' schedules, do you ask him for input? When something comes up in the family that upsets you, do you take into account that he may have a different and separate reaction than you do? When things get tough in your relationship, do you try to see things from his point of view?

When we start seeing men as appendages, we have unconsciously made them into objects. They are no longer whole, complete, separate human beings. They become "Make me happy" objects, "Make my life worthwhile" objects, "Make my life easier" objects, "You're in my way" objects, "Carry this for me" objects, "Don't humiliate me" objects, "Pay for things" objects, "Do it my way" objects, "Make me feel good about myself" objects, or "Make me look good" objects.

What to do?

If you want your man to stop taking you for granted, stop taking him for granted. To the extent that you've made him into an object that is there to fill certain needs in your life, he doesn't feel special. When he feels treated as an extension of you and your needs, he doesn't get tempted to bring you flowers or leave love notes on your pillow.

Be an inspiration by giving your man what you want from him. If you want to be thanked, thank him. If you want to be complimented, tell him what is special about him when he expresses that quality. If you want him to touch you more, give him hugs, touch his arm when you share a joke, and snuggle next to him on the sofa. If you want to have more input, ask for *his* input. Then, let him know he's pleasing you when he does something you like. He'll want more praise, and he'll be likely to do more of it.

When you can remember what it was like to cherish him and care for his needs, you can invite romance back into your relationship. When you begin caring about him as a separate person with his own desires, he will begin caring for you that way too. Someone has to go first—it may as well be you.

Ꮬ Ꮬ Ꮬ

In what ways have you been treating your man
as an object?

What would you like to see him do more of?

What could you do to inspire that?

How can you begin?

Ꮬ Ꮬ Ꮬ

Pitfall #4: Expecting him to know what I want before I do

Wouldn't it be nice if your man knew instinctively what you wanted and when to give it to you, without you having to tell him? It can seem so unromantic when he has to ask what you want. Why doesn't he *know* or *remember* when you need to be cuddled, whether you prefer silver or gold jewelry, your favorite color, when you need to be left alone, what restaurants you want to go to, and how to set the mood for seduction?

It's really easy to get annoyed with your man for being clueless about what will make you happy. Yet he is not a mind reader, and you are a complicated person who can be difficult to read and even harder to please. What you want right now may not be what you wanted yesterday—or even five minutes ago. It might not be what you want tomorrow. Your man's needs, however, probably haven't changed a whole lot since you met him. It's likely he is less complicated than you are, and this makes him easier to please. If you really want to make him happy, you probably think you know exactly what to do, right? Sometimes you're right about this and sometimes not, yet chances are you have a fairly high success rate.

Now imagine trying to make *yourself* happy from his perspective. He often feels stumped when faced with your shifting needs. He can't fathom how to give you what you want, and it makes him feel badly when he fails. Eventually, he may stop trying altogether.

Expecting your man to know what you want instinctively will leave you disappointed. If you want something, you will probably have to tell him. You may not *want* to have to tell him. It doesn't seem very romantic to have to be specific about what you want for your birthday or where you want to have that special dinner. Often, though, it's even less romantic to receive a "surprise"—because it may not be a pleasant one. Even if he's done his best to try to read your mind, he may not succeed in your eyes. If you've mentioned you like your friend's silk scarf, he might think, "Aha! I know what to get her for her birthday." When he shows up with a yellow-and-black striped wool scarf embroidered with bumblebees, he feels proud of himself. Yet it may not be what you had in mind at all! When he buys a blender for you because he heard you complain about needing a new one, he's shocked that you don't consider that the right kind of gift. He would probably *love* a gift like that.

Your man may have given up trying to give you the right gift because he felt insulted by your reception of something he gave you in the past. He might just stop altogether, or decide he'll give you what *he* would want. You have to be willing to clue him in to your desires. Then you'll likely end up with what you want. The same rule goes for emotional needs. He wants to give you what you need—yet if you don't tell him what that is, he will give you what *he* needs.

You may have to state your desires more than once. In fact, it's likely you'll have to be specific about them each time. When asking for what you want, it will be most effective to:

1. Be clear.

2. Be in a tranquil, loving place when you ask him.

3. Be willing to communicate clearly and calmly.

4. Have your heart open.

5. Be open to graciously receive what is offered.

Your man wants you to be happy. In all likelihood, when you are clear, calm, and loving in your request, he will give you what you want. Then you will be happy—and he will feel like a hero for being able to make you happy. What is more romantic than that?

❦ ❦ ❦

In what ways have you been expecting your man to read your mind?

What would happen if you could ask for what you want clearly, calmly, and lovingly?

Begin a list of what you want.

❦ ❦ ❦

Pitfall #5: Taking it personally

As human beings, we tend to think that someone else's words or actions always have something to do with *us*. After all, when we were children we believed the world revolved around ourselves, didn't we? We still have vestiges of that belief, especially when it comes to something as intimate as a relationship. As women, relationships are central to our lives. It's natural to take everything that happens in a relationship personally. Unfortunately, it can also be devastating.

When we assume everything our men say or do is related to ourselves, we make it really hard on us *and* on them. It's good for us to lean back a little and remind ourselves that our men were alive for a long time before we entered their lives. They developed habits, idiosyncrasies, and ways of doing things that have nothing to do with us. Your man is probably not doing what he does with the intent of making you unhappy. He is simply doing what he has always done.

Did you realize you may be taking things personally that may actually have very little to do with you? Think about what your response would be in the following scenarios:

1. You would like to go out to dinner, and he'd rather stay home and watch television.

2. He forgets to make plans for Valentine's Day.

3. You ask his opinion about what school to send your daughter to and he says, "You decide."

4. You want to talk through a problem and he doesn't.

It's easy to fall into thinking that everything your man does has something to do with you. If he doesn't want to go out to dinner, it must mean he's not interested anymore. If he forgets Valentine's Day, it must mean he doesn't love you. If he doesn't want to decide about the school, he doesn't care about things that really matter to you. If he doesn't want to have a deep, involved discussion about a problem, he doesn't care about your feelings. We all tend to take things personally—and it can cause a lot of mischief in our relationships.

What if instead of taking it personally when he did something, you just said, "There's my man being himself. It has nothing to do with me." When he didn't want to go out to dinner, you could think, "He must be really tired. I guess I'll call a friend and see if she wants to go out instead." Or, "He must have had a stressful day. How can I help him forget his stress and have a good evening? Maybe I'll give up my dinner plans tonight and order pizza so we can be together." When he forgot to make reservations at a restaurant for Valentine's Day, you could think, "There's my man forgetting. I guess I'll have to remind him earlier next year." When he didn't want to give an opinion about the school, you could think, "Good. I get to choose the school *I* think is best for our daughter." When he didn't want to talk through a problem in depth, you could think, "I guess this discussion is a little much for him right now. I'll bring it up again later when we're in a calmer space." Or, ask him when would be a good time and make a date to talk.

Sometimes we don't want to stop taking things personally because if we stop taking the negative things he does personally, we'll have to stop taking the positive things personally too. If he leaves love notes on the fridge, you want to think you're the only woman he's ever done that for. Yet he had other women in his life before you, right? And when he was with them he probably left them love notes, too. That doesn't mean you're not special or he doesn't mean anything by it. It just means he's a man who expresses his love by writing love notes.

If he brings you flowers...he's a flower giver.

If he doesn't bring you flowers…he's not a flower
giver.

If he compliments you…he's a compliment giver.

If he criticizes you…he's a critic.

If he does the dishes without you asking…
he's a dish doer.

If he doesn't do the dishes unless asked…
he's not a dish doer.

If he spends a lot of time with his friends…
he's a socializer.

If he wants to stay home with you every night…he's a
homebody.

If he calls you at work every day…he's a telephone
person.

If he never calls you…he's not a telephone person.

In other words, what your man does says something about *him*.
It doesn't necessarily say something about *you*. It would be worth
it to give up the positive things you take personally in order to
give up the negative things you take personally—the ones that
cause problems in your relationship. If your man does something
wonderful, by all means enjoy it. He is expressing his love for you
in the way that comes naturally to him. If he does something
that's unacceptable to you, by all means let him know. Just don't
take it personally either way. It may be difficult not to, but once
you're out of the habit you'll discover it makes your life with him
a lot smoother. You'll get your feelings hurt less, you'll start fewer
arguments, and you'll be able to relax a little more. Remind yourself often that he's with you because he loves you—and how he
acts isn't personal.

What have you been taking personally that he does?

What does that say about him?

What would happen if you stopped taking those things personally?

Pitfall #6: Not feeling desired

When you first got together with your man, sparks flew. You may not have been able to keep your hands off each other. You enjoyed feeling desirable, and you expressed your desire to him as well. Remember? Whether it's a distant memory or a recent one, there is a good chance things have changed—and you are wondering where the desire went.

It's normal that as a relationship progresses, sex may get less frequent. You may have experienced a decrease in desire. As you get familiar with him and more comfortable in your relationship, it's natural that other parts of your life together start taking over—work, kids, and household routines. Yet if he isn't quite as excited, persistent, or passionate in his overtures, your first reaction may be to take it personally. Isn't he attracted to you anymore? Why doesn't he want you all the time like he used to?

Because you're used to taking things personally and this is the most personal kind of interaction possible, of course you begin trying to find reasons for it. Who wouldn't? The problem is, the reasons you dream up tend to be self-critical, such as, "I'm not attractive," "I'm not desirable," "He's tired of me," "He doesn't want to make time for me." Criticizing yourself has you start feeling badly about yourself. You take it personally that he's not as interested, when the truth is that his reduced sex drive probably has nothing to do with you.

Yes, believe it! *Your man's reduced sex drive probably has nothing to do with whether or not he finds you attractive.* Of course he finds you attractive—he chose you! In fact, his waning interest in sex likely means that he is simply getting more comfortable with you. Men are under a lot of pressure at the beginning of a relationship to prove their virility and sexual prowess. Most men are quite concerned with making their chosen woman happy and tend to be insecure about their abilities in bed. If your man was very sexual at the beginning, part of his drive was to prove to you that he would be a good, satisfying partner for you. It may be that he used sex as a way to show his affection for you, and now he shows it in other ways.

Now that you have committed to your man, or been committed to him for a long time, he feels loved and accepted. He knows you chose him, and he no longer has such a strong need to impress you in the bedroom. He relaxes. He can put more of his energy into other parts of the relationship, his work, and his hobbies. He knows you are there for him, and he still wants you. He's just not as single-minded as he used to be. He loves you *and* he doesn't want to go to bed with you right now.

If you've been feeling badly about yourself because he doesn't take initiative as much as he used to, ask yourself:

1. Do I really want more sexual intimacy or do I want him to want it so I can feel attractive?

2. Am I using his reduced sex drive as a way to feel bad about myself?

3. Is it just easier to think he's the one who doesn't want sex, when I don't really want it either?

4. Am I using this issue as a way to push him away?

Sometimes it's easier to start feeling like a victim than to take action to change a situation. We all succumb to being the victim sometimes, especially in sensitive areas like sexual relations. It can be uncomfortable to voice your concerns to him, and it's easier to beat yourself—or him—up about it instead. The problem is that taking his reduced sex drive personally can create all kinds of problems. It's all too easy to start feeling badly about yourself, to badger him to have sex, to complain to your friends, and to cause a lot of mischief in the bedroom and your relationship.

What to do, then?

Reflect on your answers to questions #1–4 above. Determine whether you really want more sex than you're having.

If you don't want more sex, great! Remind yourself that the reason he's not all over you all the time is that he's comfortable with you and he feels accepted by you—and that you don't want it either.

If you do want more sex, inspire him. Remember, he is responding to you all the time, so you can call the shots by giving him something sensual to respond to. You know what turns him on, right? Wear something slinky or his favorite perfume, play his favorite song on the stereo, rent a sexy movie, kiss his ear, massage his shoulders.

Keep in mind that he is a separate person—not an appendage of you. He may not be able to respond in exactly the way you like, when you like it. If he had a bad day at work, it affects his libido. If he's exhausted or stressed, he may not have the energy to perform.

Be aware that issues around sex can indicate problems in other areas of the relationship. Be tender, gentle, loving, and sensual around him.

Be willing to be pleasantly surprised!

Remember, sex is probably a sensitive subject for your man, too. In fact, it may be more sensitive for him than it is for you. Men are generally more sensitive than women, particularly in any area that could question his sense of manliness. Keep your heart open to him and have compassion for his dilemma as a man in a culture that places a lot of weight on sexual prowess. Let him know how much you love and desire him—and be patient with him. He needs your reassurance as much as you need his, if not more. When you have your heart open to him and approach him with tenderness, chances are you will be able to shift the sexual dynamics in your relationship and have the sex life you desire.

ॐ ॐ ॐ

What happens when you think that his reduced sex drive has something to do with the fact that he's more comfortable with you?

Do you really want more sex, or do you just want to feel wanted?

Are you willing to go first and gently approach him in a way that works?

Can you be patient, warm, kind, and tender—and confident that you will turn this issue around?

ॐ ॐ ॐ

Pitfall #7: Being hormonal

We've all experienced moments or days when anything our man did or didn't do seemed intolerable. Yet on other days, he could do the same thing and it wouldn't bother us. Why? There may be many reasons, but it's partly because we are subject to varying degrees of hormonal fluctuation. Sometimes our mood swings can be quite volatile, overtaking us in an instant. For menstruating women, our disposition is affected by our cycles. For pregnant women, hormones can pull us all over the map. For women going through menopause, attitudes can shift drastically minute to minute or day to day.

When we don't realize that our emotional state is affected by hormonal fluctuation, our moods can cause a lot of mischief in our relationships. One woman at Life Works discovered this through playing regular tennis games with her husband. They played tennis at least three times a week, and there were certain days of the month when she became convinced he was driving the ball straight at her and trying to harm her. She would get upset, accusing him of sabotaging her game and abusing her. On other days, his aggressive serves didn't faze her in the least. Once she realized that the days she felt threatened were days she was expecting her period, she was able to deal with the situation differently. Instead of screaming at her husband, she could calmly tell him that she was feeling particularly vulnerable because she was expecting her period. She would ask him to take it easy that day and lob the ball to her gently. He was happy to comply and relieved he wouldn't be attacked anymore—and they even developed a long-standing joke about it.

It's easy to take your hormonal fluctuations for granted and forget how much they can affect the way you interpret the world. In the story in chapter 7, Florence was going through many changes. She was dealing with the "empty nest" syndrome as well as the fact that her husband was around more than he used to be. What she forgot to factor in was that she was going through the sometimes extreme changes that come with menopause. When her hormonal state was volatile, her circumstances seemed unbearable. She blamed the closest person—Neil. Things could have been quite different if instead of lashing out at him, she had enlisted his help. In order to do that, she would have had to become aware that the enormity of her upset was due in part to physical changes. It's not always easy to see this or to admit it. We would like to think we have total control over our emotions. Yet when you're upset, it's worth checking to see if you are being influenced by your hormones.

Since your man is the closest person to you, he is likely the one who takes the flak when you're feeling hormonal. Things get out of proportion, and it seems like he's the one responsible. When he's bothering you, it would be good to step back and ask yourself why his behavior seems so much more intolerable today than it did yesterday or this morning. Is he really mean and thoughtless—or are you expecting your period? Is he really the cause of all your problems—or are you experiencing a change of life? If Florence could have seen that her reaction was partly hormonal, it could have helped her open her heart to Neil and allow him to comfort her. She could have enlisted his help instead of making him the enemy.

Your man loves you, and you are a mystery to him. The more you come to understand the physical causes of your frame of mind, the more you can help him understand. Then you can have him be on your side when emotions threaten to get out of hand. Perhaps he could gently ask you if you're expecting your period. He could agree to take you out if you were too impatient to cook, or leave you on your own if you needed to be alone. Or he could help you accommodate to the body sensations brought on by menstruation, pregnancy, or menopause by giving you a massage, drawing you a bath, or putting the fan on.

Being aware of your hormones can allow you to make him your ally in dealing with the emotional ups and downs you experience. Your man knows you intimately. He is the perfect person to help you deal with the sometimes challenging changes your body experiences. He'll feel like your hero for getting you ice cream at two in the morning or taking the kids to the park when you need some time to hibernate. When you enlist his help, it can bring you closer together instead of driving a wedge between you.

☙ ☙ ☙

Think of a time recently when you were very upset at your man.

Could the enormity of your upset have been partly hormonal?

How could it have been different if you had recognized that?

☙ ☙ ☙

Pitfall #8: Missing your power

"That's it—I'm leaving!" "I've had it, I can't stand any more." "This is not working." "I'm out of here." Statements like these are threats, and they really scare your man. Why? Because he's attached to you. He's with you because he wants to be with you, and when you threaten to leave it is traumatic for him. The more macho he acts, the more it's a cover-up for how attached he is to you.

Why do we use threats? Because we think it's the only way to get what we want. We're accustomed to thinking that men aren't as attached to us as we are to them. Our culture promotes the idea that men don't want commitment, so we end up thinking they are already halfway out the door anyway. This keeps us feeling powerless, so we react strongly when things are difficult.

The fact is, your man is extremely attached to you. Because he's so attached, you can often have what you want simply by asking gently. A whisper can be more effective than a roar. When you threaten to leave, he withdraws or goes on the offensive to protect himself. When you state your needs gently but firmly, he will likely listen and be more willing to give you what you want. Saying, "I mean business" is more effective than "I'm outta here." You can't have a good relationship when one or both of you has a foot out the door.

A powerful person doesn't have to yell to be heard. When you threaten, it's because you're not aware of your own power. If you knew how powerful you were in your relationship, you'd be confident that you could have what you wanted by asking gently. Your man knows how important you are to him. Don't sabotage his trust by threatening to leave.

ॐ ॐ ॐ

Think of a time when you felt afraid your man might leave you. How did it feel?

Imagine him feeling the same way, or worse, when you threaten to leave.

ॐ ॐ ॐ

Pitfall #9: Getting gripped

Because relationships are so important to women, we tend to take them really seriously. We go into them with intensity, mentally wearing a hard hat and checking off items on a clipboard. Does he measure up? Does the relationship measure up? Are we getting everything we need? Is he loving us the way we want to be loved? Is he progressing on our timeline? The smallest detail can take on huge importance when we're analyzing it so intensely.

As we've mentioned in previous chapters, men can generally approach relationship in a lighter way. While we're busy chewing nervously on a pen and looking out for any sign of danger, they wear their party hats and carry a Frisbee. They're almost always ready to drop everything and have a little fun. That doesn't mean they don't want a serious relationship—they're just better able to roll with the punches, see the humor in it, and live in the moment rather than dwelling on the past or the future.

Why do women and men have such different attitudes toward relationship? Believe it or not, it goes all the way back to the days of the cave dwellers. In the cave times, men were usually out hunting for meat while the women were back in the cave tending the home and children. One job wasn't better than another. Men were better at hunting because of their physical strength, and women needed to be at home to bear and nurse the children. There was a clear separation of duty based on biology, and men and women needed each other to do what was necessary for survival.

On a typical day, the men would spend long periods out in the wilderness together. It took time to track their quarry or wait for it to show up. Once the animal or herd of animals appeared, the men had to be ready to engage in short spurts of intense action.

When the quarry showed itself, the men had to use their strength. They needed to be able to act spontaneously and follow the leader's orders. They had to be able to come up with a split-second strategy when the boar veered left instead of right, or when the deer came crashing at them out of the bushes. They didn't have to concern themselves much with what happened yesterday or what would happen tomorrow. They were focused entirely on the present situation.

On the other hand, while we were tending the caves we had to develop a keen sense of the past and the future. While we were bearing and nurturing the children, caring for the elderly, cultivating plants, healing the sick, resolving conflicts, cooking, and cleaning, we had to maintain a memory of what worked in the past and apply it to preparing for the future. If last year's cold winter killed off some of the tribe, we would be the ones to make sure it didn't happen again by drying extra meat and curing extra furs. Our ability to plan was a matter of life or death. Life was serious and survival was no laughing matter.

The division of labor over the course of thousands of years caused men's and women's brains to evolve differently. Men's brains were programmed to strategize, act quickly, work well within a hierarchy, be strong, and compete to be the one who won the game of survival of the fittest. Our brains were programmed to plan ahead, remember the past, keep lists of details in our minds, do many different things at once, and work cooperatively. In the caves—and more recently, in the farmhouses—this division worked to create a balance between women and men. We were relieved that they had the strength and spontaneity to do their job, and they were relieved that we had the stamina and focus to do ours. We were grateful for each other because each job was necessary for survival.

Today, the balance is different. Things have changed drastically as we entered the information age and went through the women's movement. We no longer need each other in quite the same way— yet our brains are still functioning as they were programmed to function through thousands of years of evolution. We were in the caves longer than we've been out of them, so it's natural that our biology lags behind our societal advances. Men are still programmed to go out, get the meat, protect the caves, and play ball—and we are still programmed to do everything else that needs doing.

Even when women are out in the workplace earning our living, we tend to be in charge of the household, the children, and the welfare of the family as well. Our thousands of years of experience have us well qualified for the position. We can keep grocery lists in our heads, remember our man's conference schedule, arrange car pools, plan dinners for the coming week, throw together brownies for a bake sale, care for a sick relative or child, create a comfortable space to live in, buy presents for birthdays, resolve arguments between family members....Much as we resent it sometimes because it can feel like a burden, we know we are the ones who keep the world turning.

We keep everyone fed, taken care of, and living well—and that is a serious job. Thousands of years in caves, tents, huts, and farmhouses imprinted our brains with the need to ensure survival. Yet our survival orientation today causes a lot of the small crises of life to be blown out of proportion. Every day we are making decisions that affect the well-being of the household—and those decisions often still seem like life or death to us. Somewhere in our collective experience we remember our days in the caves. We recall how if we miscalculated how much food was needed, the family would starve. Today, we could just run to the store and get more food. Yet it still seems like a matter of life or death if we run out of cranberry sauce on Thanksgiving.

Have you ever noticed how important the smallest things can seem to you? If your man lets a full gallon of milk spoil by leaving it in the car, if he accidentally drives over your newly planted flower bed, if he's late to take you to the movies, if he leaves a pile of leaves in the yard, if he announces at the last minute that he's bringing a colleague to dinner...it seems like the world is ending. We get really concerned about how, when, and where to do something because it feels like a matter of utmost urgency. When we don't realize that we're in the grip of a mostly outdated survival reaction, we tend to take it out on our men.

In the cave times, men couldn't be gripped or they couldn't act spontaneously to get meat or protect their families. Since men didn't develop that age-old grip, they tend to be a lot more relaxed about everyday decisions, mishaps, misunderstandings, or arguments. It would be good for us to learn from their more laidback attitude. Seeing how they deal with situations can help us relax as well. Since men are not programmed to worry about the past and plan for the future like we are, they trust the fact that they can act spontaneously and know what to do in the moment. They can more easily make light of a situation, joke about it, and figure out how to make it fun. They are mystified by how seriously we take it all—and they feel attacked when they bear the brunt of our urgency.

When you notice yourself getting tense, fretting about details, wanting to control everything about how the day will go, telling him the best route to take to the store…take a deep breath and lean back. Observe your man and trust that he is good at dealing with life, too—in a different way. Be willing to do things his way sometimes, and let the burden of worrying slip off your shoulders once in a while. You will enjoy more ease, and he will feel good about his ability to contribute to the relationship. You might even start having a little fun!

❦ ❦ ❦

> *What would life be like if you took your life more lightly?*
>
> *How would that affect your relationship?*
>
> *Watch your man. Notice that he loves you and can let things roll off his back.*
>
> *What can you learn from him about taking life more lightly?*
>
> *How can you help yourself loosen your grip?*

❦ ❦ ❦

Pitfall #10: Being "bored"

Life was pretty exciting when you first got together with your man, wasn't it? Every day brought new discoveries and challenges. You didn't know if you'd end up with him, and you were constantly on your toes.

Today the pace may have slowed to a walk or even a crawl. When you've been with someone for a while, that initial excitement is bound to wear off. When you've been with him for many years, it may seem that it can never come back. So what can you do to spice things up? How about a knock-down, drag-out argument every once in a while? You know what they say about make-up sex. Even a tiny misunderstanding can cause enough friction to keep things from being too mundane. But is that really the healthiest way to keep your love life juicy?

When the initial passion of attraction has cooled and everyday life settles in, it is common to begin using altercations as a way to keep the relationship spicy. Believe it or not, as you continue the work of this book and your relationship improves, you may find yourself missing the very disagreements, upsets, arguments, tensions, and fights you've been complaining about. After all, aren't we trained to think that love is dramatic? Movies, soap operas, romance novels, and torch songs tend to celebrate the tempestuous nature of passion. There's not much out there that celebrates the calm, sweet, sometimes repetitive nature of a stable relationship.

Growing to appreciate the rewards of a harmonious relationship when you are accustomed to more dramatic affairs is like learning to savor plain, unadorned foods after living on a diet of spicy, exotic dishes. If you're used to enjoying the pain and pleasure of eating the hottest vindaloo or the spiciest chile peppers, a plain carrot may not taste like anything at all at first. Yet you know you can't keep up your excessively spicy diet because it's affecting your digestion and ruining your taste buds.

Say that for the sake of your health you decide to tolerate eating bread that tastes like sawdust and vegetables that have all the flavor of pond water, because you know it's better for you in the long run. After a while, you'll notice flavors starting to sneak up on you. You begin to realize that celery tastes earthy and fresh, and that different types of bread have various sweet or sour undertones. You develop an appreciation for the subtle harmony of flavors in chicken soup or a cheese omelet. Then one day you wake up and realize you are actually craving an apple or a potato.

A happy couple is not the stuff of soap operas or romantic dramas. If Scarlett had been an adoring, supportive wife, how interested would we be in *Gone with the Wind?* Yet a loving give- and-take has a different kind of satisfaction in it—one you can learn to appreciate if you are willing to wean yourself off of a diet of drama.

Why look forward to enjoying coming home to the same man every night? Because he's the man you love, the man you chose to share your life. Because it's what you said you wanted the whole time you were single and searching. Because the deep satisfaction that comes from building a loving relationship is healthier in the long run than the thrills and heartbreak of affairs. Because if you have children or you want to have them, you and your mate need a solid, secure foundation for your family. The drama, upset, and heartbreak will lose its hold on you because once you feel the delight of a calm, supportive, loving relationship, you'll become invested in keeping it that way.

If you feel your relationship needs more spice, there are healthy things you can do that will enhance it rather than damage it. You could...

> travel to interesting places
>
> take classes
>
> work on projects together
>
> go to restaurants you love and find new ones
>
> go dancing
>
> have a regular "date night" and take turns planning

the date

read poetry to each other

go for long drives, not knowing where you'll end up

have the kids stay at a relative's or friend's house once
    a month so you can be alone together

go to theater and concerts you both enjoy

watch romantic movies together

give each other massages

have a picnic

exercise together

cook together

do volunteer work together

surprise each other

ॐ ॐ ॐ

*What have you been doing to create excitement in your
relationship that is harmful?*

What are some alternatives?

*What would it be like to have a safe space from which to go out
into the world?*

*What's the first step? Do you have any other pitfalls you slide
into in relationships? Make a list.*

*Having your own personal pitfall list can help you remember
to watch for them—and help avoid falling into them.*

ॐ ॐ ॐ

Chapter Fifteen

How to Care for You Both

IN ORDER TO FLOURISH, A CACTUS NEEDS an arid climate with warm temperatures and lots of sunlight. Ferns and moss need a cool, shady, moist forest. A palm tree needs warm tropical air and sandy soil. Each of these very different plants needs some of the same things—water, air, sunlight, and soil—but the amount and type differ. Remove any of these plants from their environment, and they will wither and perhaps even die.

Relationships, too, need a certain environment in order to be happy and healthy. What that environment looks like may be different for everyone, yet some things are constant. Just as plants need a certain amount of sunlight and water, your relationship needs a certain amount of acceptance, safety, warmth, and love. Without them, it may not be able to flourish.

Who is responsible for creating an environment for your relationship? You are. Since you are the keeper of relationship, you are the one who can cultivate a healthy space for it to thrive. That doesn't just mean what furniture or decoration you pick out for your house. It means setting an emotional tone where love can thrive.

Your mood and your attitude have everything to do with how your relationship is going. Your effect is powerful. Think about it—why do you want to be around some people and avoid others? Because of the environment they create around them. You might be drawn to people who cultivate an environment of acceptance, friendliness, fun, or tranquility. You might avoid people who cultivate an environment of exclusiveness, distance, judgment, or chaos. Whether you realize it consciously or not, you are constantly responding to people's environments—and they are responding to yours.

If you cultivate an accepting environment, you can have a relationship in which you and your man are free to be yourselves. If you cultivate an environment of tension, you can have a relationship where you're both walking on eggshells. *You* are the one with the ability to set an emotional tone that will allow a relationship to be safe, fun, tender, and loving. Your man will respond to the environment you create.

If you find it hard to believe that you're the one in charge of your relationship's environment, take a look at your friends' relationships. Can you see how the woman is the one setting the tone? Even if she seems meek and it looks like the man is the one in charge, he is constantly looking to her for clues for how to be. Men often make jokes about their wives like, "Don't ask me, ask the boss," or "We know who really wears the pants in this family." They know you are in charge of their happiness to a large extent.

CULTIVATING LOVE

Creating an environment in which your relationship can grow and thrive benefits you, your man, and your relationship. Like a garden, your relationship needs cultivation and care. And you are the gardener who can provide it. In your garden, certain things can grow and certain things can't. If your relationship is not the way you want it to be, ask yourself: What can happen in my environment?

In your environment, can your man...

> feel good about himself?
>
> feel safe?
>
> feel known?
>
> have his needs met?
>
> feel special?
>
> feel successful?
>
> feel like a hero?
>
> have his dreams come true?
>
> expect you to be on his side?
>
> want to be with you?
>
> be loving toward you?
>
> give you what you want easily?
>
> make you feel special?
>
> express his tender thoughts and feelings to you?

Following is a list of things you can do to create a wonderful environment for your relationship. Some of them you are already doing, some could use a little extra attention, and some you may want to begin cultivating.

Things to Do Every Day:

Relax about unimportant things.

Be grateful that your man is in your life.

Be grateful that he loves you.

Be complimentary.

Receive what he wants to give you...even if it is not exactly what you want.

Remind him how important he is to you.

Remember that he is different than you are.

Listen to what he has to say.

Give him the benefit of the doubt.

Let him love you.

Let him be a hero.

Things to Do Sometimes:

Give him attention in unexpected ways.

Be fun.

Be spontaneous.

Surprise him.

Ask him out on a date.

Plan fun and exciting things to do.

Get dressed up for him.

Serve him a gourmet dinner (whether you cook it yourself or not).

Do a chore he usually does that he doesn't enjoy.

Leave him love notes.

Whisper your secrets to him.

Reminisce about good times together.

Talk about things you want to enjoy with him in the future.

Be willing to…

> be pleasable
>
> get along
>
> see it his way without losing your own perspective
>
> do things his way sometimes
>
> forgive
>
> be forgiven
>
> be wrong
>
> accept his human nature
>
> like your man for who he is
>
> be a goddess in his universe

It's worth doing a little gardening every day to cultivate and maintain an environment where love can thrive. After all, you're living in your own environment all the time. You carry it around with you like a snail carrying its house on its back. Yet your environment is not static. It changes as you become more powerful and loving in your relationship. So when you are cultivating an environment for love…guess who benefits?

🍂 🍂 🍂

From a place of knowing you create your environment, ask yourself…

> *What do you do easily and well?*
>
> *In what ways can you stretch that would support your environment and therefore your relationship?*

Read the list "Things to Do Every Day."

>Select one from the list every other day that you're not
>doing that you are willing to do.

>Stretch.

Read the list "Things to Do Sometimes."

>Pick one a week to do to build up your repertoire.

Read the list "Be willing to…"

>Begin to do what you're becoming willing to do.

Look forward to noticing your man's response to you as you
cultivate a loving environment.

Observe his response to:

>your caring

>your appreciation

>your understanding

>your giving him the time he needs to express himself

>your ability to see his view as valid and precious

Be open to feeling the love flowing between you.

>When you notice it, breathe into the moment,

>letting the good feelings permeate your heart and your body.

Allow yourself to continue being open and loving,

>listening to him and caring for him.

✒ Care and Feeding Manuals

What conditions do *you* need in order to flourish mentally, physically, and emotionally? Your body, mind, and emotions need a certain kind of care that's unique to you. Giving your man a "Care and Feeding" manual about you is a fun and helpful way for him to know you better. Why not make it as easy as possible for him to make you happy?

A sample manual might include instructions like the following:

Don't ask me questions in the morning until I've had my first cup of coffee.

If you have something important to discuss with me, wait until the evening—but make sure you bring it up before ten o'clock.

When I get cranky at four o'clock in the afternoon, it means I need a snack—but don't give me sweets. A piece of cheese or fruit is perfect.

I sometimes criticize my parents, but I get upset if you criticize them.

My favorite time for cuddling is early morning.

I get edgy if I don't exercise at least three times a week.

When I do something I feel badly about, it's hard for me to apologize aloud. I tend to say I'm sorry by giving flowers or writing a note.

When I'm stressed about work, I need to complain—but I'm not necessarily looking for solutions.

I need an hour of alone time every day.

Following is a sample "Care and Feeding" manual for you to fill in. You can use it or create your own manual. Write about what you know about yourself, then show it to your man. Sharing it with him shows him you care and you're interested in him. Your man will love knowing what really makes you happy. He *wants* to be your hero.

CARE AND FEEDING MANUAL

for_____

(Name)

The most important thing to know about me is...

_____

Wake me in the morning by...

_____

When I wake up in the morning, I like...

_____

When I'm going to bed at night, I like...

_____

In order to have a good night's sleep, I need...

_____

Times I like to be quiet are...

_____

Times I like to be alone are...

_____

Times I like to be social are...

_____

My ideal evening in is...

_____

My ideal evening out is...

_____

Ideally, I'd stay in ___ nights per week and
        go out ___ nights per week.

Chores I like to do are...

_____

Chores I don't mind doing if I have to are...

_____

Chores I hate doing are...

_____

Chores I refuse to do are...

_____

I like to take care of the following things by myself:

_____

I like someone else to take care of the following things for me:

_____

When I get tired, I...

_____

When I get hungry, I...

_____

When I need exercise, I...

_____

When I need a break, I...

_____

When I need inspiration, I...

_____

When I'm at a loss for what to do, I...

_____

In a crisis, I...

_____

On my birthday, I like...

_____

On my birthday, I don't like...

_____

On anniversaries, I like...

_____

On anniversaries, I don't like...

_____

For the holidays, I like...

_____

For the holidays, I'd rather not...

_____

When I'm entertaining guests at home, I...

_____

At a party, I...

_____

When I'm sick, I need...

_____

When I'm anticipating a stress-producing event, I need...

_____

When I'm around my family, I...

_____

When I'm complaining about someone or something, I need...

_____

When I need time alone, I...

_____

When I'm lonely, I...

_____

The best thing you can do for me at that time is...

_____

What makes me angry is...

_____

When I'm feeling angry, I...

_____

The best thing you can do for me when I'm feeling that way is...

_____

What makes me sad is...

_____

When I'm feeling sad, I...

_____

The best thing you can do for me when I'm feeling that way is...

_____

What hurts me is...

_____

When I'm feeling hurt, I...

_____

The best thing you can do for me when I'm feeling that way is...

_____

What scares me is...

_____

When I'm feeling afraid, I...

_____

The best thing you can do for me when I'm feeling that way is...

_____

What humiliates me is...

_____

When I'm feeling humiliated, I...

_____

The best thing you can do for me when I'm feeling that way is...

_____

What gives me joy is...

_____

When I'm feeling joyful, I...

_____

The best thing you can do for me when I'm feeling that way is...

_____

My favorite time to have sex is...

_____

A time I rarely want to have sex is...

_____

What helps get me in the mood is...

_____

What really gets me out of the mood is...

_____

If I'm cranky in the morning I might need...

_____

If I'm cranky in the afternoon I might need...

_____

If I'm cranky in the evening I might need...

_____

I need time to myself when...

_____

When I'm upset, I tend to...

_____

What I need when I'm upset is...

_____

I tend to handle stress by...

_____

When I get stressed out, please do...

_____

When I get stressed out, please don't...

_____

When I'm menstruating, please do...

_____

When I'm menstruating, please don't...

_____

I hate it when others...

_____

I hate it when I...

_____

Please feel free to call me on it if I...

_____

Please walk on eggshells around me (and don't bring it up till
     later) if I...

_____

Things people say that can really set me off are:

_____

Things people do that can really set me off are:

_____

When I say,   "_____",

     I really mean, "_____."

When I say, "_____",

     I really mean, "_____."

When I say, "_____",

     I really mean, "_____."

When I say, "_____",

I really mean, "_____."

"Good" habits I have are...

_____

"Bad" habits I have are...

_____

Anything else I'd like you to know about me is...

_____

✒ Allowing Your Relationship to Flourish

Here's a quick list designed to help you navigate the daily waters of your relationship. The information is compiled from concepts in the book to provide a convenient reference for you. It would be good to go over this list once in a while to remind yourself what you've learned about how your man is, what it works for you to do, and why you're spending so much effort on your relationship in the first place.

Do Nots

Do not blame or criticize him. That doesn't mean he's never at fault or he doesn't do things to provoke your anger. It means that blaming and criticizing him will not get you what you want. Remember that he's extremely sensitive to your criticism. He will resort to "bad boy" behavior when he feels attacked. That means he'll go away, break a promise, or pick a fight with you later about something seemingly unrelated.

Do not approach him with anger. When you are upset, find a way to let out your anger that doesn't involve him. Hit a pillow, talk to a friend, write in a notebook, go for a run...whatever you need to do to get the anger out. Then discuss it with him. Since he responds more to your tone of voice than your words, it's important to be calm when you have something to say. He'll be more able and willing to hear you and help you find a solution. If he feels under attack, he will not be likely to give you what you want. You won't get your needs met or have it your way.

Do not insist on being right. It's hard to be wrong. Of course you want to be right, but it's worth letting go of the need to be right all the time. When you're holding on fiercely to being right, he is forced to hold on to his side just as fiercely. You'll go around and around in your argument and probably won't end up with a satisfactory solution.

Do not be careless about how you speak. When you're angry, you rarely end up saying what you mean. You leave things out and say things you regret or slant your request in a hurtful way. It's good for you to think through what you want to say and then say it flatly, in a matter-of-fact way. When you're willing to be wrong and have it be different, you will be open to hearing your man's side of the issue. He responds well to you when he feels heard and understood. When you're allowing him space to be right, he will be far more likely to listen to your side, too. When you feel fierce about being right, ask yourself, "Do I want to be right or do I want to be happy?" or "Do I want it my way or do I want to be happy?"

Do not assume you know him better than he knows himself. You don't. It's insulting to him when you disregard his reality and insist you know better. You wouldn't want him to do that to you, would you?

Do not humiliate him. This may take some attention on your part. He gets humiliated easily. Even your tone of voice might be enough to humiliate him. And certainly don't do any of the following in public: directly contradict something he says, get in a "right-wrong" debate, or tell a story that demeans him. It's not worth the repercussions that will come later. It *is* worth it to make him look great in the eyes of others. He will feel like a hero and will want to do anything for you.

Do not compare him to an ideal. He'll never measure up—how can he? Comparing him to an ideal will only keep you dissatisfied. It won't bring out the best in him, either. How can he shine when he knows he doesn't measure up?

Do not treat him as an object. He's a real, live, walking, talking, breathing human being. Get to know him as someone separate from yourself. You may be surprised at his hidden depths, and he will be grateful that you are willing to know and accept him for who he is. He will be relieved that you're taking his needs into consideration and not assuming he's an appendage of you.

Do not take it personally. He cares about you or he wouldn't be with you. Assume that he's on your side and that he's not intentionally hurting you. He has upsets that have nothing to do with you. There is almost always another explanation than "He doesn't love me" or "He's trying to hurt me." Remember that he is who he is, and you just happen to be in his life. He didn't create who he is especially for you.

Do

Love him. Open your heart to him. He is longing for you to love him wholeheartedly. When you feel yourself closing off to him, do the exercise "Warming Your Heart" on page 131. When you approach your man in an open, loving, accepting way, he will respond in kind.

Love yourself. He wants you to be happy. He knows the key to his happiness lies in yours. "Happy wife, happy life." So do what it takes to nurture and care for yourself. When you're healthy, well-rested, calm, and involved in activities that you enjoy, you both benefit.

Be aware of the effect you have. Keep in mind that how you are matters to your man. Your mood sets the tone for the relationship. When you're constantly worried about how he is affecting you, you are forgetting that you are also affecting him. When you are in charge of your effect, you have power in your relationship.

Watch out for pitfalls. When things go downhill fast, it may be that you've fallen into one of the common relationship pits. Then it's time to reread the "Pitfalls" section—and go over your personal "Pitfalls" list.

Notice the environment you are creating. He responds well to a safe, caring, accepting environment. He does not respond well to a critical, blaming environment.

Remember he is different than you are. He is not like you and your girlfriends. He's bigger, hairier, and simpler. In short, he is a man. He appreciates it when you understand him and don't expect him to be like you. He'll behave well when he feels accepted and understood.

Be willing to stand in his shoes. Keep in mind that his reality is different from yours. It is just as real to him as yours is to you. When you don't understand where he's coming from, try standing in his shoes for a while. It looks different from where he's standing, doesn't it?

Be willing to go first. When you want something to shift, you are the one who can do it. He *wants* you to do it. He knows you are the keeper of the relationship and he's looking to you for leadership. He will follow your heartfelt example.

Help him make you happy. Learn to be pleasable. Being pleasable means having the ability to accept what he gives you, no matter what it looks like. It means looking in a way that allows you to see first the love with which he gives it to you, and then the gift itself. It means being nice and not always having to get it your way. It means accepting his way of loving you with gratitude. If you want something different, let him know gently what it is. Then acknowledge him when he gives it to you—even if it's not exactly what you had in mind. He wants to be your hero. Let him.

Be patient. Change takes time, and it may be a while before he begins responding differently to you. Don't try to rush it. Let it take the time it takes.

Enjoy the day in and day out. A loving relationship is not always exciting. When you have your hearts open to each other and treat each other well, there's not a lot of drama. You may miss that, but it's a good thing to learn to tolerate its absence. Don't give in to the urge to create mischief just to shake things up a bit.

Cherish him and treat him tenderly. He will respond in kind.

What You Can Look Forward To

Your relationship is a tender bond between the two of you. You can have it be the way you want it to be. It doesn't have to look like your parents' relationship, his parents' relationship, or anyone else's relationship. You don't even have to know how you want it to be as long as you are open to making it up as you go along. You can have it be the way you want it, and you can both have your needs met as long as you honor your relationship and hold it as something sacred.

It will all happen, it's just a matter of time. Things are going to shift now. They probably already are. As you experience the opening and warming of your heart and your man's response to it, and as you use all the new skills you've learned, expect that it will become wonderful—and that it may still be difficult sometimes. No one is waving a magic wand, and humans tend to resist change. That doesn't mean it's not happening—it just may take longer than you wish it would.

Some changes will happen in a day, some in a week, and some in a year. You can conceive of a change in an instant, yet making the change can take some time. Be willing to let the changes unfold as they will. Keep in mind that the changes may be subtle, and be open to noticing when something has shifted. Trust that as you shift, your man will shift too—just as when you move an object in space, the other objects around it have to shift to accommodate it.

If you lose faith, do the following: Put your hand on your heart, breathe, and remind yourself that things take the time they take. Life doesn't always happen on your time schedule. Yet things happen when they are ready to happen. In hindsight, it's hard to remember your impatience—and the time you had to wait for change seems worth it.

BE WILLING TO TAKE A STEP BACK
AND REMEMBER THAT...

You are two people who are each wonderful in your own right.

You are two people who chose each other as partners.

You are two people who may have loosened or lost your connection to each other.

You are two people living in two separate realities.

You are two people who have your own histories that formed you.

You are two people who have a history together.

You are two people who have each made mistakes.

You are two people who may have miscommunicated.

You are two people who want to find a solution.

You are two people who may be scared something will get lost if you give in or let yourself be vulnerable.

You are two people learning to end the argument by saying, "I see my part and I'm sorry."

You are two people who would rather be loving each other than upset with each other.

You are two people who are working to understand each other.

You are two people who can remember you love each other.

You are two people who want to be willing to do what works.

You are two rough stones tumbling together through the stream of life.

Above all, don't forget to acknowledge yourself for the extraordinary shifts you're making. What you are doing takes courage, willingness, patience, strength—and most of all—love. Remember that you *can* have what you want that is good for you, your man, your family, and your friends. Your willingness to open your heart will allow you to be cherished in the way you deserve. It can happen, it's just a matter of time.

We wish you a full, openhearted experience of life. We are cheering for you as you learn to have the love and tenderness you desire. You are worth the time and attention it may take to be cherished. Congratulations...you are well on your way.

AFTERWORD

The more you live this work, the more you will become an expert at being cherished. You will become an inspiration for other women to heal, grow, shift, open their hearts, and have the relationship they want. Women will look to you as an example. The more you are willing to share with them, the more you will broaden and deepen your own experience of relationship.

We hope you will become a mentor for other women. We have seen how powerful it can be to help other women through the experience of our Guidesses, whose gentle mentoring has helped so many women to have more of what they want. Each Guidess grows in her own experience as she mentors others.

Sometimes women get together to complain about men. When we do that, it increases our discontent and takes us further away from the possibility of being cherished. Now you have the opportunity to be a catalyst for change by helping other women open their hearts. Sharing your experience of becoming cherished will also help the planet because it will be increasing the love and understanding between women and men. It is our intention that the world becomes a place where more of us can be cherished...one woman at a time.

EXERCISE LIST

BIBLIOGRAPHY

Bradshaw, John. *Creating Love: The Next Great Stage of Growth.* New York: Bantam Doubleday Dell, 1993.

Breathnach, Sarah Ban. *Romancing the Ordinary: A Year of Simple Splendor.* New York: The Simple Abundance Press, 2002.

Carlson, Richard, and Benjamin Shield, eds. *Handbook for the Heart: Original Writings on Love.* Boston: Little, Brown & Co., 1996.

Chopra, Deepak. *The Path to Love: Spiritual Strategies for Healing.* New York: Three Rivers Press, 1997.

Dass, Ram. *The Only Dance There Is.* New York: Doubleday & Co., Inc., 1974.

Deida, David. *It's a Guy Thing: An Owner's Manual for Women.* Deerfield Beach, FL: Health Communications, Inc., 1997.

Dowrick, Stephanie. *Forgiveness and Other Acts of Love.* New York: W. W. Norton & Co., 1997.

Godek, Gregory J. P. *Love: The Course They Forgot to Teach You in School.* Naperville, IL: Casablanca Press, 1997.

———. *1001 Ways to Be Romantic.* Naperville, IL: Casablanca Press, 2000.

Gottman, John, Ph.D., with Nan Silver. *Why Marriages Succeed or Fail...and How You Can Make Yours Last.* New York: Simon & Schuster, 1994.

Gray, John, Ph.D. *Men Are from Mars, Women Are from Venus: A Practical Guide for Improving Communication and Getting What You Want in Your Relationships.* New York: HarperCollins, 1992.

———. *Mars and Venus Together Forever: Relationship Skills for Lasting Love.* New York: HarperPerennial, 1996.

Gyatso, Tenzin, the Fourteenth Dalai Lama. *The Compassionate Life.* Boston: Wisdom Publications, 2001.

Hendricks, Gay, Ph.D., and Kathlyn Hendricks. *Conscious Loving: The Journey to Co-Commitment—A Way to Be Fully Together Without Giving Up Yourself.* New York: Bantam Books, 1990.

Jampolsky, Gerald G., M.D., and Diane V. Cirincione. *Love Is the Answer: Creating Positive Relationships.* New York: Bantam Books, 1990.

Kantor, David, Ph.D. *My Lover, Myself: Self-Discovery Through Relationship.* New York: Riverhead Books, 1999.

Lerner, Harriet, Ph.D. *The Dance of Connection: How to Talk To Someone When You're Mad, Hurt, Scared, Frustrated, Insulted, Betrayed, or Desperate.* New York: Quill, 2001.

Louden, Jennifer. *The Couple's Comfort Book: A Creative Guide for Renewing Passion, Pleasure & Commitment.* San Francisco: HarperSanFrancisco, 1994.

Losoncy, Dr. Lewis E. *If It Weren't for You, We Could Get Along!: How to Stop Blaming and Start Living.* Sanford, FL: DC Press, 2001.

Luskin, Dr. Fred. *Forgive for Good: A Proven Prescription for Health and Happiness.* San Francisco: HarperSanFrancisco, 2002.

Ornish, Dean. *Love and Survival: 8 Pathways to Intimacy and Health.* New York: HarperCollins, 1999.

Paleg, Kim, Ph.D., and Matthew McKay, Ph.D. *When Anger Hurts Your Relationship: 10 Simple Solutions for Couples Who Fight.* Oakland, CA: New Harbinger Publications, Inc., 2001.

Spezzano, Chuck, Ph.D. *If It Hurts, It Isn't Love—and 365 Other Principles to Heal and Transform Your Relationships.* New York: Marlowe & Co., 1991.

Tannen, Deborah, Ph.D. *That's Not What I Meant!: How Conversational Style Makes or Breaks Relationships.* New York: Ballantine Books, 1986.

Weiner-Davis, Michele. *Divorce Busting: A Revolutionary and Rapid Program for Staying Together.* New York: Summit Books, 1992.

Westheimer, Dr. Ruth. *Dr. Ruth's Guide for Married Lovers.* New York: Warner Books, 1992.

Williamson, Marianne. *A Return to Love: Reflections on the Principles of "A Course in Miracles."* New York: HarperCollins, 1996.

ACKNOWLEDGMENTS

We wish to thank all the graduates of Life Works Workshops since we began in 1984 who have each used their wisdom, time, flexibility, and energy to have their relationships support them in the work they are each contributing to our world.

The Life Works Guidesses who are a source of support and an example of our work together in New York: Patty Accarino, Carole Forman, Lisa Gilpin, Paula Kramer Weiss, Sue Krevlin, Sara Lustigman, Sylvia Moss, Miriam Nelson-Gillett, Anne Prather, Gloria Waldman-Schwartz, Peg Warren, Cheryl Marks Young, and Marion Yuen. And those across the country: in Boston, Cathy Petter; Dallas, Susan Lockard and Chris Shull-Caldera; Charlotte, North Carolina, Nancy Schreiber; Philadelphia, Cathy Ellich-Owen; San Francisco, Barbara Blair-Dallosto; and Santa Fe, Debra Cox. We also thank the women of the Guidess Training Intensive, who are following in their footsteps.

Heartfelt thanks to the team who helped create this book: wordsmiths Elizabeth Law and Suzanne Lander, clarifier Jeff Braucher, artist John Buse, communicator Eileen Duhne, and Ellen Kleiner and Pat Walsh-Haluska for their good advice and wisdom. We thank our early readers for their insights: Liz Bard, Pamela Benson, Colleen Cleary, Debra Cox, Iris Feldman, Beth Greer, Sue Harrison, Micki Langloys, Susan Lockard, Linda Musso, Peg Warren, Susan Walsh, and Melissa Weisstuch.

To our parents Frances and Maxwell Graman, Michael and Rosemary Walsh, and Catherine Todd and Walter Erston, and to our families who provided us with our first experience of being treasured.

And finally to the cherishing men in our lives, our husbands, the late Vishnu Lee Jayson and the always generous Bill Speers, and fiancé Joey Palombi for helping us learn to warm and open our hearts.

ABOUT THE AUTHORS

Marilyn Graman is a psychotherapist with a thriving practice in Manhattan's Greenwich Village. She began working with clients in 1978 and in 1984 she and Maureen Walsh founded Life Works, Inc., offering workshops, seminars, retreats, and intensives. Dedicated to helping people have more of what they want in life, Life Works has developed a curriculum of courses for women and men to teach and support the process of creating and living an invigorating, fulfilling, and meaningful life.

A graduate of Queens College with a Masters degree in early childhood education from City University, Marilyn says she learned most of what she knows about human beings in her 12 years as a kindergarten teacher in New York City.

Marilyn was happily married to Vishnu Jayson until his sudden death in 1995. A resident of Fire Island's Fair Harbor and Manhattan's Fifth Avenue, she travels extensively, studying what it means to be human around the world.

❦

Maureen Walsh is called a business therapist by her clients and is the cofounder of Life Works, Inc. No stranger to walking in many worlds, Maureen earned an undergraduate degree in art history and held graduate fellowships in the theatre department and business school, while studying for her marketing MBA.

Maureen's extensive work in the arts included managing The Philadelphia Theater Company, The Children's Theater Company in Minneapolis, the Brooklyn Academy of Music, and the Joffrey Ballet. Her subsequent work in advertising grew into her own consulting firm helping New York artists and healers evolve into successful business owners.

A producer at heart, Maureen guides the development of new

projects, creates and delivers specialized courses, and is the business side of Life Works. She and her husband live in Santa Fe and Los Angeles.

※

Hillary Welles grew up in Ithaca, New York, and northern Vermont. She received her Bachelor of Arts in English from Smith College in 1991, and a Master of Arts in 1993 from the University of Birmingham's Shakespeare Institute in Stratford-upon-Avon in England. Upon her return to the United States, she developed a successful violin studio in Vermont, and another in Santa Fe, New Mexico, where she now resides.

In 2000 Hillary gave up her violin career for her true passion—writing. She has cowritten three self-help books with Marilyn and Maureen.

Would you like to have your own Guidess?

You are invited to call Life Works to set up an appointment to speak with a Guidess, one of the wise women who you read about in the book. Our staff of well-trained women practitioners were called Coaches until several years ago, but the term never fit the delicate and profound work they do. So we invented a new word that we feel more clearly describes the powerful Guiding that they do at Life Works.

Guidesses have completed a three-year training program and are prepared to personally assist you in moving toward what you want by providing weekly support or giving more focused attention on short term issues. The Guidesses are experts in the Life Works technology and point-of-view. They can partner with you as you begin uncovering and clearing what is in your way, having a stronger, more loving relationship with yourself, clarifying what you want, and gracefully receiving it as it flows into your life.

The Life Works Guiding staff was trained and is supervised by Marilyn and Maureen, and they assist women, men, and couples in private confidential sessions on a weekly or biweekly basis. They work both in our New York offices and by telephone to your office or home. The 45-minute sessions are offered at reasonable rates (currently from $40–$85 per session).

We will be glad to assist you in selecting the right Guidess. People who have not completed a Workshop begin with a half-hour intake consultation with our Guidess Coordinator to discuss issues and find the right Guidess match.

If you have been looking to do some work on yourself with a gentle, clear, openhearted, well-grounded woman of wisdom, please call tollfree 877-741-8787 to set up an appointment.

THE COURSE THAT INSPIRED THIS BOOK
HOW TO BE CHERISHED
A Weekend Workshop from Life Works

Remember how you glowed when you were first in love with your man? People loved being around you because you radiated happiness. The love you shared with your man made life seem good, and you were sure you'd be happy forever. Marilyn Graman will reassure you that you can have a luscious relationship again...and it can be even better than ever before.

It is natural for relationships to have an ebb and flow, to grow more or less intimate as circumstances shift. Relationships need care and nurturing, and often it's hard to know what to do. This Workshop is designed to offer gentle and insightful guidance—whether you need to perk up an already good relationship, find answers to how to solve particular issues, resolve a crisis, decide whether to stay or go, learn from a past relationship so this one works, reconnect with your man, or recover from heartbreak and be ready for your next relationship.

You have probably been searching for reasons why your relationship isn't as warm, loving, and tender as you'd like. Marilyn knows how difficult that can be, and is happy to tell you that you don't have to do it all on your own anymore. She will help guide you to find the real reasons why your relationship might not be all you desire—and you may be surprised at what you find.

Marilyn will help you see that there's nothing wrong with you...that in fact, you are far more powerful in your relationship than you ever imagined. She will help you learn to use your power for yourself...so you can have the happy, luscious, exciting, accepting, fun, caring relationship you desire. Not only is it possible, it's closer than you would believe. You can have it, you deserve it...and she will guide you there. We'll help you get the glow back and feel cherished again.

The How to Be Cherished Workshop hours are from 9:30 to 7pm both Saturday and Sunday and the fee is $495. If you would like to join us for a weekend, call 877-741-8787 to enroll.

WE HELP YOU MAKE YOUR DREAMS COME TRUE...

In the heart of Greenwich Village in downtown Manhattan, Marilyn Graman, Maureen Walsh, and their staff invite you to learn and practice the art of creating and living an invigorating, fulfilling, meaningful life. A place where you can explore who you are meant to be.

The curriculum at Life Works focuses on the basics—relationships, career, and having more power in your life—in weekly support groups as well as weekend courses and longer retreats and intensives. Underlying all the courses is the conviction that with time, attention, and support, it is possible to unburden your life of the things that haven't been working, while bringing in the things that will give your life more joy, ease, and satisfaction. Through these courses, bright, vibrant, successful people like you are finding a way to more fully express themselves and their own unique nature.

Life Works, Inc.,
55 Fifth Avenue – Penthouse
New York, NY 10003
212-741-8787
tollfree 877-741-8787   fax 212-741-9242

Visit our web site at www.lifeworksgroup.com

Join us at Life Works and create a life you're glad to wake up to.

Life Works is the home of:

WORKSHOPS

Having What You Want With a Man Weekend*

Life Works! Workshop

How to Be Cherished*

The Natural Power of Being a Woman*

The Money Workshop

How to Make a Graceful Living

Reboot Your Life—Preparing for the Second Half

ONGOING GROUPS

The Gathering*

Relationship Support Group*

Money Support Group

RETREATS

Mother*, Father*

Clearing the Path

Manifestation

INTENSIVES

Guidess Training Program*

Female Power Within Leadership Program*

Marriage Works*

SEMINARS

Free and open to both Graduates and guests on the
2nd Wednesday of most months

GUIDING PROGRAM (formerly Coaching)

Reasonable rates for individual support in your life

*for women only

BOOKS FROM LIFE WORKS

The Female Power Within and *There Is NO PRINCE* are the first two books in a series based on the workshops and seminars we've developed at Life Works since 1984. Our workshops and our books are designed to help women and men discover their authentic power so they can have more of what they want in all areas of their lives.

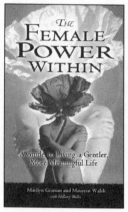

The Female Power Within

A Guide to Living a Gentler,
More Meaningful Life

"Imagine a world in which every woman has the opportunity and encouragement to be herself—a world where success is not measured by how many deals you make or whether or not you have children, but by how authentically you are living."

Thus begins this breakthrough book on discovering and living from your authentic power.

The Female Power Within outlines a step-by-step process for coming to know yourself intimately and deeply. Through deep questioning, meditations, exercises, and visualizations, this how-to manual encourages women to rediscover the perceptions, patterns, pleasures, and power of being female.

"The Female Power Within *is a groundbreaking exploration of the nature of women's power. It reveals that our power is in our authenticity. It is time to stop being angry with men, and stop being limited by them. As more women uncover their true natures we will, as Marilyn and Maureen suggest, transform the world."*

—ARIANNA HUFFINGTON
syndicated columnist and author

"The Female Power Within *is a beautifully written guidebook to help you tap into the inner reservoir of peace and joy that is your true nature."*

—SRI SWAMI SATCHIDANANDA
Integral Yoga Institutes & Centers

"I know from personal experience that Marilyn and Maureen's empowering concepts and techniques work. They've created an exciting and meaningful contribution to the worldwide shift occurring in women today. If you're serious about self-discovery, read this book!"

—BETH GREER
President, The Learning Annex

Enhance and Empower Your Life!

There Is NO PRINCE is an invitation to women of all ages to get crystal clear about what matters most to them in a man, and to celebrate their own power and potential. As this warm, insightful, and clear-headed relationship guidebook so ably demonstrates, there may not be any Princes, but there are millions of wonderful men out there who want to make them happy.

There is NO Prince
and Other Truths
Your Mother Never Told You:

A Guide to Having
the Relationship You Want

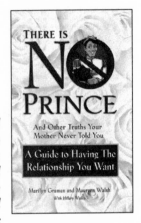

"Every woman deserves a man who can stand behind her and applaud as she blossoms. She deserves a man who can be a best friend, consort, cheerleader, listener, cuddler, financial partner, father to her children, companion, and fellow traveler—a man who is an asset to her life. Every woman deserves to have a man who supports her and cherishes her. In short, every woman deserves to have the relationship she wants."

Thus begins this wise guide that takes you step-by-step through the process of preparing for a 21st-century relationship.

There Is NO PRINCE overturns old ideas and conventional thinking about relationships. Based on our popular "Having What You Want With a Man" workshop, *There Is NO PRINCE* reminds women, single and partnered, that we have the power to change what we attract and to shape our relationships to have what we want. For the first time in book form, Marilyn reveals secrets from our workshop that have helped even the most die-hard skeptics find relationship bliss.

"Every woman who is disappointed with her love life needs to read this informative and practical book. The authors gently open our eyes to the unconscious beliefs we hold that have us repeating the same old mistakes over and over. Best of all, we're shown how to love and honor ourselves as we're given guidelines to attracting a relationship that will really work for us."

—Louise Hay
author of *You Can Heal Your Life*
and *Empowering Women*

"There is NO PRINCE *is a practical and illuminating guidebook for women in all stages of relationship."*

—John Gray, Ph.D.
Author of Men Are from Mars, Women Are from Venus

More resources from Life Works Books

How to Be Cherished
  —A Guide to Having the Love You Desire
                              $22.95 x_____ =_____

There Is NO PRINCE
and Other Truths Your Mother Never Told You
  —A Guide to Having the Relationship You Want
                              $22.95 x_____ =_____

The Female Power Within
  —A Guide to Living a Gentler,
    More Meaningful Life

                              $22.95 x_____ =_____

The Female Power Within
  Meditations and visualizations from the book
  Audio Tape $10.00 x_____ =_____

"What is the most loving thing
  I can do for myself now?"
  Heart magnets $2.00 x_____ =_____

                    Subtotal $_____
Tax (New York residents add 8.25%) $_____
            Shipping and handling $_____
            Add $2.95 for first item
      and $1.00 for each additional item
                  Total enclosed $_____

        Make checks or money orders to:
        Life Works Books,
        55 Fifth Avenue – Penthouse
        New York, NY 10003

Watch your bookstore for new Life Works Books releases. Contact us at the address above if you would like to receive our mailings or email us at www.lifeworksbooks.com.